Phrase**Guide**

MANDARIN

With menu decoder, survival guide and two-way dictionary

Thomas Cook
Publishing

www.thomascookpublishing.com

Survival guide.................49

Emergencies.....................59

Dictionary.........................63

Quick reference................95

How to use this guide

The ten chapters in this guide are colour-coded to help you find what you're looking for. These colours are used on the tabs of the pages and in the contents on the previous page and above.

For quick reference, you'll find some basic expressions on the inside front cover and essential emergency phrases on the inside back cover. There is also a handy reference section for numbers, measurements and clothes sizes at the back of the guide.

Front cover photography © Jon Arnold Images/Alamy
Cover design/artwork by Jonathan Glick
Photos: Ljubisa Bojic (p14), Jon Connell (p25), Dreamstime.com
[Guodingping (p59), Ilustrator79 (p11), Jameslee (p18), Linqong (p28),
Loveasmoke (p41), Anton Malikov (p58), Monkey Business Images (p19),
Zhudifeng (pp49 & 50)], M Forman (pp9 & 10), Romain Guy (p62),
Hanhanpeggy (p12) and Kevin Tuck/SXC.hu (p43).

Produced by The Content Works Ltd
Aston Court, Kingsmead Business Park, Frederick Place
High Wycombe, Bucks HP11 1LA
www.thecontentworks.com
Design concept: Mike Wade
Layout: Alison Rayner
Text: Jill Thomas
Editing: Paul Hines
Proofing: Monica Guy & Wei Xue
Editorial/project management: Lisa Plumridge

Published by Thomas Cook Publishing
A division of Thomas Cook Tour Operations Limited
Company registration No: 3772199 England
The Thomas Cook Business Park, 9 Coningsby Road
Peterborough PE3 8SB, United Kingdom
Email: books@thomascook.com, Tel: +44 (0)1733 416477
www.thomascookpublishing.com

ISBN-13: 978-1-84848-106-0

First edition © 2009 Thomas Cook Publishing
Text © 2009 Thomas Cook Publishing

Series Editor: Maisie Fitzpatrick
Production/DTP: Steven Collins

Printed and bound in Italy by Printer Trento

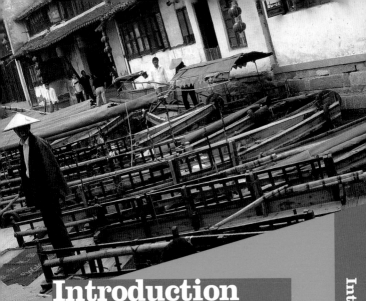

Introduction

Mandarin is spoken by over a billion people. Now, it wouldn't be so popular if it was difficult, so forget everything you thought you knew about it being tricky – it's not: it's actually easier than English. The Chinese know that Westerners are sometimes in awe of the language, and any effort you make with it will impress them mightily.

So give it a go! As the philosopher Lao Tzu said, "The journey of a thousand leagues begins with a single step". This guide will help you take that single step – and quite a few more – easily, enjoyably and gracefully.

Although it traces its roots back over 3,000 years, the Chinese language of Mandarin is relatively new: it wasn't until the early 20th century that a unified tongue evolved, and this was called Putonghua (now better known as Mandarin). In their written form, its words are individual characters. Outside of Hong Kong and Taiwan, you're likely to encounter the simplified characters that we're using in this guide.

The basics

There are two aspects to speaking Mandarin: pronunciation and tones. The former is made easy by pinyin, the system used to transcribe it into our alphabet. Generally speaking, Brits don't have much difficulty with pronunciation as most of the sounds are similar to English; just remember to soften your vowels. For example, with *bàn* (半, half), say *bahn* instead of *ban*.

It's the tones that most find slightly tricky. There are four of these, which are represented as marks above each vowel in pinyin.

Tone	Pinyin example	Description	Character	Translation
1st	*bā*	High and steady	八	eight
2nd	*bá*	Rising from mid-level to high	拔	to uproot

Saying it right

There are differences between English and pinyin. One example is "c", which sounds like the *ts* in *hits*. So *cǎo* (草, grass) is pronounced *tsao*. With vowels, "e" sounds like the *er* in *her*, so *chē* (车, car) is pronounced *cher*. There's also ü, which doesn't exist in English but sounds like the French "u" (as, for example, in *lune*). Try saying *ee-oo* really quickly with your lips pouted.

3rd	*bǎ*	Starting low, dipping then rising	把		to hold
4th	*bà*	Falling from high to low	爸		father
Neutral *ba*		Flat, with no emphasis	叭		trumpet

The untrained ear will have trouble distinguishing these tones, but keep trying.

Grammar

Mandarin employs the same basic sentence structure as English: subject-verb-object. For example:

我	爱	我的	狗
wǒ	*ài*	*wǒ de*	*gǒu*
I	love	my	dog

To ask a question, insert the question word ("where", "who", "what", "how", "why") where the answer would go:

洗手间	在哪里?
xǐ shǒu jiān	*zài nǎ lǐ?*
Toilet	where? (Where's the toilet?)

洗手间	在里面
xǐ shǒu jiān	*zài lǐ miàn*
Toilet	inside (The toilet is inside)

One of the big pluses about Mandarin is that there are no tenses, so you don't have to worry about conjugating the right verb. Instead, whether something is past, present or future is determined from the context of the sentence. Another good thing is that there are no articles ("a", "an" or "the"), which means no fiddly genders or plurals with nouns. 餐馆 (*cān guǎn*, restaurant) could refer generally to a restaurant or restaurants, or to a specific restaurant. The sentence will provide contextual clues.

Basic conversation

Hello	你好	*nǐ hǎo*
Goodbye	再见	*zài jiàn*
Yes	是的	*shì de*
No	不是	*bú shì*
Please	请	*qǐng*

Thank you	谢谢	*xiè xie*
You're welcome	不用谢	*bú yòng xiè*
Sorry	对不起	*duì bu qǐ*
Excuse me (apology)	对不起	*duì bu qǐ*
Excuse me (to get attention)	请问	*qǐng wèn*
Excuse me (to get past)	请让一下	*qǐng ràng yī xià*
Do you speak English?	你说英语吗?	*ní shuǒ yīng yǔ ma?*
I don't speak Mandarin	我不会说普通话	*wǒ bú huì shuō pǔ tōng huà*
I speak a little Mandarin	我只说一点普通话	*wǒ zhǐ shuō yī diǎn pǔ tōng huà*
What?	什么?	*shén me?*
I understand	明白	*míng bǎi*
I don't understand	我不明白	*wǒ bù míng bǎi*
Do you understand?	你明白吗?	*ní míng bǎi ma?*
I don't know	我不知道	*wǒ bù zhī dào*
I can't	我不能	*wǒ bù néng*
Can you... please?	你能...一下吗?	*nǐ néng... yī xià ma?*
- speak more slowly	– 慢慢讲	- *màn man jiǎng*
- repeat that	– 重复	- *chóng fù*

Cultural crossovers

To the distress of purists, English expressions are creeping into Mandarin, mainly as slang among the young. To say goodbye, instead of *zài jiàn* (再见), you might hear people saying *bāi bái* (拜拜).

Greetings

The Chinese are fairly reserved, so a handshake and a nod are enough when you are introduced to a new person. You might also see someone giving a slight bow or lowering their eyes on first meeting; these are gestures of respect.

Common variations on greetings are *chī le ma?* (吃了吗?, Have you eaten?) and *shàng nǎ er?* (上哪儿?, Where are you going?). Answering *chī le* (吃了, I've eaten) and *chū qù le* (出去了, I'm going out) will suffice.

Keep body contact to a minimum – if you're getting on well with someone, a friendly pat on the back is okay, but hugs and kisses are out.

Meeting someone

Hello/Hi	你好	*nǐ hǎo*
Good morning	早晨好	*zǎo chén hǎo*
Good afternoon	下午好	*xià wǔ hǎo*
Good evening	晚上好	*wǎn shàng hǎo*
Sir/Mr	先生	*xiān shēng*
Madam/Mrs	女士	*nǚ shì*
Miss	小姐	*xiǎo jiě*
How are you?	你好吗?	*nǐ hǎo ma?*
Fine, thank you	很好，谢谢	*hěn hǎo, xiè xie*
And you?	你呢?	*nǐ ne?*
Very well	很好	*hěn hǎo*
Not very well	不太好	*bú tài hǎo*

Title tricks

It's polite to address people, especially those you don't know, as *xiān shēng* (先生, Sir), *nǚ shì* (女士, Madam) or *xiǎo jiě* (小姐, Miss). If in doubt about a woman's age, plump for the safer *xiǎo jiě* option.

Small talk

My name is...	我叫...	*wǒ jiào...*
What's your name?	你叫什么名?	*nǐ jiào shén me míng?*
I'm pleased to meet you	很高兴认识你	*hěn gāo xìng rèn shì nǐ*
Where are you from?	你从哪里来?	*nǐ cóng nǎ lǐ lái?*
I am from Britain	我从英国来	*wǒ cóng yīng guó lái*
Do you live here?	你住在这里吗?	*nǐ zhù zài zhè lǐ ma?*
This is a great...	这个...	*zhè gè... zhēn liǎo bù qǐ*
	真了不起	
- country	- 国家	*- guó jiā*
- town	- 城市	*- chéng shì*

I am staying at...	我住在...	*wǒ zhù zài...*
I'm just here for the day	我要呆一天	*wǒ yào dài yì tiān*
I'm in China for...	我在中国要呆...	*wǒ zài zhōng guó yào dài...*
- a weekend	– 一个周末	*- yí gè zhōu mò*
- a week	– 一个星期	*- yí gè xīng qī*
How old are you?	你多大年纪了?	*nǐ duō dà nián jì le?*
I'm... years old	我... 岁	*wǒ... suì*

Family

This is my...	这是我的...	*zhè shì wǒ de...*
- husband	– 丈夫	*- zhàng fu*
- wife	– 妻子	*- qī zi*
- partner	– 朋友	*- péng you*
- boyfriend/ girlfriend	– 男朋友/女朋友	*- nán péng you/ nǚ péng you*

I have a...	我有一个...	*wǒ yǒu yí gè...*
- son	– 儿子	*- ér zi*
- daughter	– 女儿	*- nǚ ér*
- grandson	– 孙子	*- sūn zi*
- granddaughter	– 孙女	*- sūn nǚ*

Do you have...	你有... 吗?	*nǐ yǒu... ma?*
- children?	– 孩子	*- hái zi*
- grandchildren?	– 孙子	*- sūn zi*
I don't have children	我没有孩子	*wǒ méi yǒu hái zi*

Are you married?	你结婚了吗?	*nǐ jié hūn le ma?*
I'm...	我...	*wǒ...*
- single	– 单身	*- dān shēn*

The name game
With Chinese names, the surname comes first and the given name can have two components: someone called Li Wen Rong should be referred to as Mr Li.

- married	- 结婚了	- *jié hūn le*
- divorced	- 离婚了	- *lí hūn le*
- widowed	- 寡居	- *guǎ jū*

Saying goodbye

Goodbye	再见	*zài jiàn*
Good night	晚安	*wǎn ān*
Sleep well	睡个好觉	*shuì ge hǎo jiào*
See you later	一会儿见	*yí huì er jiàn*

Have a good trip!	一路平安	*yí lù píng ān*
It was nice meeting you	认识你很高兴	*rèn shì nǐ hěn gāo xìng*
All the best	一路顺风	*yí lù shùn fēng*
Have fun	希望你玩好	*xī wàng nǐ wán hǎo*
Good luck	祝你好运	*zhù nǐ hǎo yùn*
Keep in touch	保持联系	*bǎo chí lián xì*

| My address is... | 我的地址是... | *wǒ de dì zhǐ shì...* |
| What's your... | 你的... 是什么? | *nǐ de... shì shén me?* |

- address?	- 地址	- *dì zhǐ*
- email?	- 电子邮件	- *diàn zǐ yóu jiàn*
- telephone number?	- 电话号码	- *diàn huà hào mǎ*

Saying yes, nicely

If someone is showering you with compliments, feign humility and reply *nǎ lǐ, nǎ lǐ* (哪里,哪里; not true, not true). Invitations should be accepted with grateful declarations of being thrilled but not wanting to put anyone out.

Eating Out

If your only experience of Chinese food is from the corner takeaway, you're in for a real treat.

Chinese food is wonderfully diverse, from the seafood dishes of the southern coast to the fiery cuisine of the inner provinces. Indeed, ingredients and styles of cooking vary tremendously from region to region.

You'll find plenty of dining places to choose from. Grab a snack from a roadside stall, or nip into a modest eatery for a quick bowl of noodles. And if you have time and cash to spare, a multi-course Chinese banquet is the only way to go.

Introduction

To the Chinese, food is more than just fuel, it's a way for people to express care and concern for (and socialise with) their family and friends.

Some roadside stalls and small restaurants might look dingy, but don't let this put you off – the priority is hygiene, not surface appearances.

Unfortunately, most Chinese restaurants aren't very veggie-friendly, but it is possible to find vegetarian restaurants, especially near or at Buddhist temples.

I'd like...	我想要...	*wǒ xiǎng yào...*
- a table for two	– 一张两人的桌子	*- yì zhāng liǎng rén de zhuō zǐ*
- a sandwich	– 三明治	*- sān míng zhì*
- a coffee	– 咖啡	*- kā fēi*
- a tea (with milk)	– 茶（加奶）	*- chá (jiā nǎi)*
Do you have a menu in English?	你是否有英语菜单？	*nǐ shì fǒu yǒu yīng yǔ cài dān?*
The bill, please	请给我账单	*qǐng gěi wǒ zhàng dān*

You may hear...

吸烟区还是禁烟区？	*xī yān qū hái shi jìn yān qū?*	Smoking or non-smoking?
你想吃什么呢？	*nǐ xiǎng chī shén me ne?*	What are you going to have?

Like clockwork

Mealtimes are punctual and the Chinese eat fairly early, with lunch at noon and dinner at 6 or 7pm. Many kitchens stop serving after 8 or 9pm, even in large cities.

Dim sum, and then some

Dim sum, or 点心 (*diǎn xīn*) is a meal comprising lots of small snack-like dishes. A typical dim sum meal will include dumplings – with prawns, pork or vegetables – buns, rolls and an array of other goodies, steamed or fried.

The cuisines of China

National specialities

Chinese meals usually have two components: the main base of the meal, which can be rice, noodles, buns or pancakes; and the accompanying meat and vegetables. Rice dishes are more common in the south; wheat-based noodles and buns are usually found further north.

Signature dishes (see the menu decoder for more dishes)

炒饭	*chǎo fàn*	Fried rice
粥	*zhōu*	Rice porridge
面汤	*miàn tāng*	Noodles in soup
云吞	*yún tūn*	Wonton
粽子	*zòng zi*	Glutinous rice wrapped in bamboo leaves
包子	*bāo zi*	Filled steamed buns
馒头	*mán tóu*	Plain steamed buns

Cantonese

As most Chinese restaurants in the UK are based on the Cantonese tradition, this style will be familiar to many. The use of fresh ingredients is essential. These are often stir-fried or steamed with minimal seasoning to bring out their flavours.

Signature dishes (see the menu decoder for more dishes)

冬瓜汤	*dōng guā tāng*	Winter melon soup
焖鲍鱼	*mèn bào yú*	Braised abalone
咕唠肉	*gū lǎo ròu*	Sweet and sour pork

豉椒排骨	*chǐ jiāo pái gǔ*	Steamed spare ribs
叉烧	*chā shāo*	Barbecued roast pork
烧鹅	*shāo é*	Roast goose

One for all
Chinese dining is a communal affair, where each person gets their own bowl of rice and all the other dishes are placed in the middle of the table and shared. This is why food usually comes in bite-sized pieces.

Szechuan

The food from this region uses a lot of chillies and spices. and tends to rely more on preserved – pickled, salted, smoked or dried – ingredients. A unique item is the Szechuan peppercorn, which has a citrus flavour and momentarily numbs the mouth.

Signature dishes (see the menu decoder for more dishes)

酸辣汤	*suān là tāng*	Hot and sour soup
宫保鸡丁	*gōng bǎo jī dīng*	Spicy chicken and peanuts
回锅肉	*huí guō ròu*	Double-cooked pork
樟茶鸭	*zhāng chá yā*	Tea-smoked duck
麻婆豆腐	*má pó dòu fu*	Spicy tofu with minced meat
麻辣茄子	*má là qié zi*	Spicy aubergine

Northern

Wheat, not rice, is the staple grain here, and more unconventional meats, including mutton and goat, are also a feature. Think hearty fare for protection against the harsh climate. Beijing cuisine, which evolved from imperial culinary tradition, is more diverse.

Signature dishes (see the menu decoder for more dishes)

| 叉烧酥 | *chā shāo sū* | Barbecued pork in flaky pastry |
| 北京烤鸭 | *běi jīng kǎo yā* | Peking duck |

木须肉	*mù xū ròu*	Sliced stir-fried pork with vegetables
富贵鸡	*fù guì jī*	Beggar's chicken (baked and stuffed chicken)
烤羊肉	*kǎo yáng ròu*	Roast lamb
锅塌豆腐	*guō tā dòu fu*	Sautéed tofu

Eastern

Slow cooking is the name of the game: stews and braised dishes are common. This is where you'll find the famous "red cooking", where slow simmering in soy sauce, sugar and flavoursome spices gives the meat a dark-reddish tinge.

Signature dishes (see the menu decoder for more dishes)

臭豆腐	*chòu dòu fu*	Fermented tofu
小笼包	*xiǎo lóng bāo*	Pork- and soup-filled dumplings
醉鸡	*zuì jī*	Wine-marinated steamed chicken
狮子头	*shī zi tóu*	Large pork meatballs
红烧牛肉	*hóng shāo niú ròu*	Soy sauce braised beef
炒年糕	*chǎo nián gāo*	Stir-fried rice cakes

Licking your chop(stick)s

Chinese meals are eaten with chopsticks. Never leave them standing vertically in a bowl of rice or noodles, as this symbolises death.

Wine, beer & spirits

The brewing tradition goes back millennia, while liquors are typically wheat- or rice-based. Local beers are a must-try, and some of them can put hair on the proverbial chest. Winemaking is also taking off.

黄酒	*huáng jiǔ*	Yellow liquor
白酒	*bái jiǔ*	Distilled liquor
葡萄酒	*pú tao jiǔ*	Wine (from grapes)
啤酒	*pí jiǔ*	Beer
玫瑰露酒	*méi guī lòu jiǔ*	Rose essence liquor
竹叶青酒	*zhú yè qīng jiǔ*	Bamboo leaf liquor

Slow and steady
Chinese alcoholic drinks can be hot or cold. They are especially nice warm, as this brings out their depth. With an alcohol content ranging from 15 to 65 per cent, they're more to be sipped than guzzled.

You may hear...

你想要什么?	*nǐ xiǎng yào shén me?*	What can I get you?
你想要怎么熟?	*nǐ xiǎng yào zén me shú?*	How would you like it?
加冰或无冰?	*jiā bīng huò wú bīng?*	With or without ice?
冷或温烧的?	*lěng huò wēn shāo de?*	Cold or room temperature?

Snacks & refreshments

The comparative lightness of some Chinese food can lead to Western visitors feeling like they need the occasional in-between-meal snack. Luckily, in China it is common to 'graze' – topping up the tank throughout the day with various nibbles. Even better, locating sources of refreshment does not require much effort: you'll find numerous street stalls selling tempting steamed buns and dumplings.

肉包	ròu bāo	Meat-filled buns (usually pork)
油条	yóu tiáo	Fried dough sticks
开口笑	kāi kǒu xiào	Sesame seed balls
杏仁豆腐	xìng rén dòu fu	Almond tofu
蜂糕	fēng gāo	Steamed honey cake
拔丝山药	bá sī shān yào	Candied yams

Vegetarians & special requirements

I'm vegetarian	我是素食者	wǒ shì sù shí zhě
I don't eat...	我不能吃...	wǒ bù néng chī...
- meat	– 肉	- ròu
- fish	– 鱼	- yú
Could you cook something without meat in it?	你能做无肉的餐吗?	nǐ néng zuò wú ròu de cān ma?
What's in this?	里面是什么?	lǐ miàn shì shén me?
I'm allergic to...	我对... 过敏	wǒ duì... guò mǐn

Children

Are children welcome?	我们可以带儿童吗?	wǒ men ké yǐ dài ér tóng ma?
Do you have a children's menu?	你是否有儿童菜单?	nǐ shì fǒu yǒu ér tóng cài dān?
What dishes are good for children?	你能给儿童推荐什么?	nǐ néng gěi ér tóng tuī jiàn shén me?

Kiddie corners
Finding a child-friendly restaurant won't be difficult. Some have open kitchens where you can see chefs making dumplings or pulling noodles from huge lumps of dough – guaranteed to keep the little ones fascinated.

Menu decoder

Essentials

Breakfast	早餐	*zǎo cān*
Lunch	午餐	*wǔ cān*
Dinner	晚餐	*wǎn cān*
Cover charge	附加费	*fù jiā fèi*
VAT included	包括商品增值税	*bāo kuò shāng pǐn zēng zhí shuì*
Service included	包括服务费	*bāo kuò fú wù fèi*
Credit cards (not) accepted	(不)接受信用卡	*(bú) jiē shòu xìn yòng kǎ*
First course	开胃菜	*kāi wèi cài*
Second course	主菜	*zhǔ cài*
Dessert	甜饼	*tián bǐng*
Dish of the day	当日菜	*dāng rì cài*
Local speciality	当地特色菜	*dāng dì tè sè cài*
House specials	主厨特餐	*zhǔ chú tè cān*
Set menu	固定价格菜单	*gù dìng jià gé cài dān*
A la carte	按菜谱点菜	*àn cài pǔ diǎn cài*
Tourist menu	游人菜单	*yóu rén cài dān*
Wine list	酒水单	*jiǔ shuǐ dān*
Drinks menu	饮料单	*yǐn liào dān*
Snack menu	小吃菜单	*xiǎo chī cài dān*

Fabulous feasts

Chinese banquets can be lavish affairs, so be an emperor for a day and treat yourself to a sumptuous slap-up meal. Dishes usually come in this order: appetisers, soup, seafood, white meat, red meat, vegetables, rice or noodles and dessert.

Street meats
You'll pass countless roadside vendors selling snacks and other exotic goodies cooked up right in front of you. These can be anything from sweets and buns to kebabs, wontons and fried insects.

Methods of preparation

Baked	烤	*kǎo*
Boiled	煮	*zhǔ*
Braised	焖	*mèn*
Breaded	裹面粉	*guǒ miàn fěn*
Deep-fried	油炸	*yóu zhá*
Fresh	新鲜	*xīn xiān*
Fried	油煎	*yóu jiān*
Frozen	结冰	*jié bīng*
Grilled/broiled	烤	*kǎo*
Marinated	卤汁	*lǔ zhī*
Mashed	泥	*ní*
Poached	水煮	*shuǐ zhǔ*
Raw	生	*shēng*
Roasted	烤	*kǎo*
Salty	咸	*xián*
Sautéed	炒	*chǎo*
Smoked	熏	*xūn*
Spicy (flavour)	有味	*yǒu wèi*
Spicy (hot)	辣	*là*
Steamed	蒸	*zhēng*
Stewed	炖	*dùn*
Stuffed	有馅	*yǒu xiàn*
Sweet	甜	*tián*
Rare	三分熟	*sān fēn shú*
Medium	五分熟	*wǔ fēn shú*
Well done	全熟	*quán shú*

Common food items

Beef	牛肉	*niú ròu*
Chicken	鸡肉	*jī ròu*
Turkey	火鸡	*huǒ jī*
Lamb	小羊肉	*xiǎo yáng ròu*
Pork	猪肉	*zhū ròu*
Fish	鱼	*yú*
Seafood	海鲜	*hǎi xiān*
Tuna	金枪鱼	*jīn qiāng yú*
Beans	豆子	*dòu zi*
Cheese	乳酪	*rǔ lào*
Eggs	鸡蛋	*jī dàn*
Lentils	扁豆	*biǎn dòu*
Pasta/noodles	面团/面条	*miàn tuán/miàn tiáo*
Rice	大米	*dà mǐ*
Aubergine	茄子	*qié zi*
Cabbage	圆白菜	*yuán bái cài*
Carrots	胡萝卜	*hú luó bo*
Cucumber	黄瓜	*huáng guā*
Garlic	蒜	*suàn*
Mushrooms	蘑菇	*mó gū*
Olives	橄榄	*gǎn lǎn*
Onion	葱	*cōng*
Potato	土豆	*tǔ dòu*
Red/green pepper	红/绿柿子椒	*hóng/lǜ shì zi jiāo*
Tomato	番茄	*fān qié*
Vegetables	蔬菜	*shū cài*
Bread	面包	*miàn bāo*
Oil	油	*yóu*
Pepper	胡椒粉	*hú jiāo fěn*
Salt	盐	*yán*
Vinegar	醋	*cù*

Missed manners
You may encounter surly waiters and waitresses. Don't let this ruin your enjoyment of the food; regard it as part of the experience!

Cake	蛋糕	*dàn gāo*
Cereal	麦片粥	*mài piàn zhōu*
Cream	奶油	*nǎi yóu*
Fruit	水果	*shuǐ guǒ*
Ice cream	冰淇凌	*bīng qi líng*
Milk	牛奶	*niú nǎi*
Tart	馅饼	*xiàn bǐng*

Some like it hot

A local favourite is hot pot, a broth whose possibilities are endless: veggies, tofu, eggs and noodles can all go in. At the end, you get a beautifully mellow soup flavoured by everything that's been cooked.

Popular sauces

酱油	*jiàng yóu*	Soy sauce
苏梅酱	*sū méi jiàng*	Plum sauce
蚝油	*háo yóu*	Oyster sauce
芥末	*jiè mo*	Mustard
蛋黄酱	*dàn huáng jiàng*	Mayonnaise
蒜蓉豆豉酱	*suàn róng dòu chǐ jiàng*	Black bean sauce
XO 酱	*XO jiàng*	XO sauce
辣油	*là yóu*	Chilli oil

Appetisers

泡菜	*pào cài*	Pickled vegetables
春卷	*chūn juǎn*	Spring rolls
虾片	*xiā piàn*	Prawn crackers
皮蛋	*pí dàn*	Preserved egg
凉拌海蜇皮	*liáng bàn hǎi zhé pí*	Jellyfish strips
卤牛肉	*lǔ niú ròu*	Chilled stewed beef
蒸饺	*zhēng jiǎo*	Steamed dumplings

Soups

| 鱼丸汤 | *yú wán tāng* | Fishball soup |
| 贡丸汤 | *gòng wán tāng* | Meatball soup |

蛋花汤	*dàn huā tāng*	Egg and vegetable soup
玉米蛋汤	*yù mǐ dàn tāng*	Sweetcorn and egg soup
紫菜汤	*zǐ cài tāng*	Seaweed soup
馄饨汤	*hún tun tāng*	Wonton soup
肉羹汤	*ròu gēng tāng*	Thick pork soup
豆腐汤	*dòu fu tāng*	Tofu soup

Seafood dishes

蒸鲈鱼	*zhēng lú yú*	Steamed sea bass
油炸虾	*yóu zhá xiā*	Deep-fried prawns
蒜蓉蒸扇贝	*suàn róng zhēng shàn bèi*	Steamed scallops with garlic
炒海参	*chǎo hǎi shēn*	Sautéed sea cucumber
焖鲍鱼	*mèn bào yú*	Braised abalone
姜葱龙虾	*jiāng cōng lóng xiā*	Lobster steamed with ginger and spring onions
姜葱炒蟹	*jiāng cōng chǎo xiè*	Crab fried with ginger and shallots
油炸鱿鱼丸	*yóu zhá yóu yú wán*	Deep-fried squid balls

Meat dishes

| 铁板牛肉 | *tiě bǎn niú ròu* | Sliced beef on a hot plate |

Niblets and giblets
Tripe, feet, ears and other parts of the animal that aren't usually palatable to Brits are fairly commonplace. If you're not feeling adventurous, ask 是肉吗? (*shì ròu ma?*, Is this meat?).

干煸牛肉丝	gān biān niú ròu sī	Crispy fried beef strips
黑胡椒牛肉	hēi hú jiāo niú ròu	Black pepper beef
腰果鸡丁	yāo guǒ jī dīng	Chicken and cashew nuts
四川炸鸡	sì chuán zhá jī	Szechuan-style deep-fried chicken
软炸鸡条	ruǎn zhá jī tiáo	Breaded chicken strips
宫保肉丁	gōng bǎo ròu dīng	Spicy pork with peanuts
鱼香肉丝	yú xiāng ròu sī	Spicy pork with vegetables
京酱肉丝	jīng jiàng ròu sī	Stir-fried pork in a mildly sweet sauce
孜然羊肉	zī rán yáng ròu	Pan-fried spicy lamb

Tackling touts

You may encounter restaurant touts, pushy characters who shove a menu in your face, invite you in to "look", and then sit you down and bring you some appetisers before you can even blink. If you don't like what you're seeing, just walk away.

Tofu dishes

家常豆腐	jiā cháng dòu fu	Homestyle tofu
麻辣豆腐	má là dòu fu	Spicy tofu
青椒豆腐干	qīng jiāo dòu fu gān	Tofu strips stir-fried with green peppers
炸豆腐	zhá dòu fu	Fried tofu
沙锅豆腐	shā guō dòu fu	Tofu braised in a clay pot
锅贴豆腐	guō tiē dòu fu	Fried tofu stuffed with fish
皮蛋豆腐	pí dàn dòu fu	Minced tofu with pickled eggs
熘豆腐	liū dòu fu	Sautéed tofu

Vegetable dishes

蒜蓉绿花菜	suàn róng lǜ huā cài	Stir-fried broccoli with garlic
烧芸豆	shāo yún dòu	Stir-fried green beans
清蒸白菜	qīng zhēng bái cài	Steamed bok choy
地三鲜	dì sān xiān	Stir-fried potatoes, green peppers and aubergine
烧荷兰豆	shāo hé lán dòu	Stir-fried snow peas
炸茄盒	zhá qié hé	Breaded aubergine stuffed with meat
鱼香茄条	yú xiāng qié tiáo	Spicy stir-fried aubergine
蚝油生菜	háo yóu shēng cài	Lettuce stir-fried in oyster sauce
烧白菜	shāo bái cài	Fried Chinese cabbage
六合菜	liù hé cài	Six seasonal vegetables, stir-fried

Crunch time

If you're vegetarian, do tell the waiter (but you'll still have to be on guard for bits of meat or dried prawn). Thankfully, there are some great vegetarian restaurants.

Rice and noodle dishes

肉末菠菜	ròu mò bō cài	Spinach with minced pork
米饭	mǐ fàn	Plain rice
蛋炒饭	dàn chǎo fàn	Egg fried rice
水饺	shuǐ jiǎo	Boiled pork dumplings
锅贴饺子	guō tiē jiǎo zi	Fried pork dumplings

担担面	dàn dàn miàn	Spicy stir-fried noodles
蛋炒面	dàn chǎo miàn	Egg-fried noodles
肉炒面	ròu chǎo miàn	Pork-fried noodles
牛肉面	niú ròu miàn	Beef-fried noodles
云吞面汤	yún tūn miàn tāng	Wonton noodles with soup

Top tipple

Tea – usually either jasmine or chrysanthemum – is the beverage of choice at a Chinese meal. It's thought to complement the flavours of the food, and to neutralise any oiliness in the dishes.

Desserts

水果	shuǐ guǒ	Mixed fruit
夹沙香蕉	jiā shā xiāng jiāo	Stuffed bananas
拔丝苹果	bá sī píng guǒ	Caramelised apple chunks
拔丝香蕉	bá sī xiāng jiāo	Caramelised banana chunks
八宝饭	bā bǎo fàn	Rice pudding with "eight treasures" (fruit and nuts)
红豆沙	hóng dòu shā	Sweet red bean pudding
花生小甜饼	huā shēng xiǎo tián bǐng	Mini peanut tart
雪面豆烧	xuě miàn dòu shāo	Rice balls with red bean filling

Drinks

茉莉花茶	mò lì huā chá	Jasmine tea
绿茶	lǜ chá	Green tea
乌龙茶	wǔ lóng chá	Oolong tea
菊花茶	jú huā chá	Chrysanthemum tea

果汁	guǒ zhī	Juice
纯净水	chún jìng shuǐ	Mineral water
可口可乐	kě kǒu kě lè	Coca-cola
雪碧	xuě bì	Lemonade
芬达	fēn dá	Fanta
汽水	qì shuǐ	Fizzy drink
豆奶	dòu nǎi	Soy milk

Snacks

方便面	fāng biàn miàn	Instant noodles
蛋饼	dàn bǐng	Custard tart
煎饼	jiān bǐng	Pancake
切糕	qiē gāo	Glutinous rice cake
花糕	huā gāo	Rice cake with bean paste
栗子糕	lì zi gāo	Chestnut cake with bean paste
凉粉	liáng fěn	Bean jelly
麻花	má huā	Fried dough twists

A timeless tradition

Teahouses are a great way to soak up a little local culture and rest your tired feet. Most serve snacks as well. These can be dumplings, sweet or savoury pastries, or dessert puddings. You'll get to sample as much of the local brew as you want, as top-ups are usually free.

Shopping

From bustling markets to swanky new shopping malls, China has enough to keep any shopaholic satisfied. There are great bargains to be had, and if you want weird and wonderful, head for a flea market to hunt for Communist memorabilia, art or just something unusual.

For a touch of the Orient, choose from the array of jade or pearl jewellery you'll find in shops and markets across China. Most visitors also find it hard to resist the silks and beautifully embroidered linens, all of which make great gifts to take home.

Essentials

Where can I buy...?	哪里能买...?	*nǎ lǐ néng mǎi...?*
I'd like to buy...	我想买...	*wǒ xiǎng mǎi...*
Do you have...?	你有... 吗?	*nǐ yǒu... ma?*
Do you sell...?	你卖... 吗?	*nǐ mài... ma?*
I'd like this	我要了	*wǒ yào le*
I'd prefer...	我比较喜欢...	*wǒ bǐ jiào xǐ huān...*
Could you show me...?	你能让我看看... 吗?	*nǐ néng ràng wǒ kàn kan... ma?*
I'm just looking, thanks	我只是看看	*wǒ zhǐ shì kàn kan*
How much is it?	多少钱?	*duō shǎo qián?*
Could you write down the price?	你能把价钱写下来吗?	*nǐ néng bǎ jià qián xiě xià lái ma?*
Do you have any items on sale?	有打折的物品吗?	*yǒu dǎ zhé de wù pǐn ma?*
Could I have a discount?	能打折吗?	*néng dǎ zhé ma?*
Nothing else, thanks	就这些, 谢谢	*jiù zhè xiē, xiè xie*
Do you accept credit cards?	你接受信用卡吗?	*nǐ jiē shòu xìn yòng kǎ ma?*
It's a present: could I have it wrapped, please?	它是礼物: 你能把它包裹吗?	*tā shì lǐ wù: nǐ néng bǎ tā bāo guǒ ma?*
Could you post it to...?	你能把它托运去... 吗?	*nǐ néng bǎ tā tuō yùn qù... ma?*

The art of haggling

In China, bargaining is expected. Before you enter the fray, have an idea of how much you're willing to pay. Find out what the seller is asking, offer between one-fifth and one-quarter and work your way to a final deal.

Can I exchange it?	我想换一个	*wǒ xiǎng huàn yí gè*
I'd like to return this	我想退回	*wǒ xiǎng tuì huí*
I'd like a refund	我想退款	*wǒ xiǎng tuì kuǎn*

Pearl jammin'
Beware of imitation pearls, which are made from glass or plastic and then coated. To tell real ones from fakes, rub the pearl against your teeth. Real pearls feel slightly sandy; fake ones are smooth.

Local specialities

In addition to jade and pearls, jewellery made from lacquer and *cloisonné* is also popular. These traditional crafts beautify vases, dishes and other decorative items.

Tea aficionados will be in heaven here, as there are numerous tea salons with rooms for quaffing and experts who are more than happy to discuss the intricacies of the different blends.

Can you recommend a shop selling local specialities?	你能推荐卖当地特产的店吗?	*nǐ néng tuī jiàn mài dāng dì tè chǎn de diàn ma?*
What are the local specialities?	当地特产是什么?	*dāng dì tè chǎn shì shén me?*
What should I buy from here?	这里有什么好买?	*zhè li yǒu shén me hǎo mǎi?*
Is this good quality?	品质是优良吗?	*pǐn zhì shì yōu liáng ma?*
Do you make this yourself?	是你自己制造的吗?	*shì nǐ zì jǐ zhì zào de ma?*
Is it handmade?	是手工制造吗?	*shì shǒu gōng zhì zào ma?*
Do you make it to measure?	你能定制吗?	*nǐ néng dìng zhì ma?*
Can I order one?	我能发订单吗?	*wǒ néng fā dìng dān ma?*

Popular things to buy

The best bargains to be had are in speciality ceramics or jewellery shops, where you'll find beautiful crafts without the hefty import markup that's slapped on them in stores back home. Common souvenirs include terracotta warrior replicas, kites and calligraphy kits for the kids, and, more recently, Olympic memorabilia. You can also pick up some propaganda from the Cultural Revolution era, like posters, satchels and little red books.

古董	*gǔ dǒng*	antiques
书法用品	*shū fǎ yòng pǐn*	calligraphy supplies
筷子	*kuài zi*	chopsticks
翡翠	*fěi cuì*	jade
风筝	*fēng zhēng*	kites
漆器	*qī qì*	laquerware
珍珠	*zhēn zhū*	pearls
瓷器	*cí qì*	porcelain
陶器	*táo qì*	pottery
丝绸	*sī chóu*	silk
中国画	*zhōng guó huà*	traditional paintings

The stuff of legends

Many of the items in antiques markets aren't really that old – some may have even been caked in mud to appear aged. Genuine items are more likely to be found in speciality shops.

Clothes & shoes

Clothing, particularly silk, is generally much cheaper in China. Markets and local shopping plazas have every imaginable item of clothing, from socks to jumpers and coats. But be aware that if a designer brand is being sold for next to nothing, it's definitely fake. For something classier, check out Shanghai Tang, a homegrown chain with a luxurious collection of Chinese-inspired clothing, accessories and gifts.

| Where is the... department? | ...部在哪里? | ... *bù zài nǎ li?* |

Friends forever
Friendship stores, or
友谊商店 (yǒu yì shāng diàn)
are state-owned boutiques
originally set up to cater
to foreign residents and
tourists. They're good
places to pick up high-
quality items, including
souvenirs and silks.

- clothes	– 服装	- fú zhuāng
- shoes	– 鞋	- xié
- women's	– 女士的	- nǚ shì de
- men's	– 男士的	- nán shì de
- children's	– 儿童的	- ér tóng de
Which floor is the...?	...在几楼?	... zài jǐ lóu?

I'm looking for...	我想要...	wǒ xiǎng yào...
- a skirt	– 裙子	- qún zi
- trousers	– 长裤	- cháng kù
- a top	– 女衬衫	- nǚ chèn shān
- a jacket	– 夹克	- jiá kè
- a T-shirt	– T恤衫	- tī xù shān
- jeans	– 牛仔裤	- niú zǎi kù
- shoes	– 鞋子	- xié zi
- underwear	– 内裤	- nèi kù

Can I try it on?	我能试穿吗?	wó néng shì chuān ma?
What size is it?	这件衣服是多大号?	zhè jiàn yī fu shì duō dà hào?
My size is...	我穿...	wǒ chuān...
- small	– 小号	- xiǎo hào
- medium	– 中号	- zhōng hào
- large	– 大号	- dà hào

(see clothes size converter on p96 for full range of sizes)

Do you have this in my size?	有我的尺寸吗?	yǒu wǒ de chǐ cùn ma?
Where is the changing room?	试衣间在哪里?	shì yī jiān zài nǎ li?

It doesn't fit	不合适	*bù hé shì*
It doesn't suit me	不适合我	*bù shì hé wǒ*
Do you have a... size?	你有... 一点的吗?	*nǐ yǒu... yì diǎn de ma?*
- bigger	– 大	- *dà*
- smaller	– 小	- *xiǎo*

Do you have it/them in...	有... 的吗?	*yǒu... de ma?*
- black?	– 黑色	- *hēi sè*
- white?	– 白色	- *bái sè*
- blue?	– 蓝色	- *lán sè*
- green?	– 绿色	- *lǜ sè*
- red?	– 红色	- *hóng sè*

Are they made of leather?	是皮革吗?	*shì pí gé ma?*
I'm going to leave it/them	我不要了	*wǒ bú yào le*
I'll take it/them	我要了	*wǒ yào le*

Fits like a glove

For bespoke clothing, ask a local contact or at your hotel for a recommended tailor. Go with a specific idea in mind of what you want. If you can, take an example with you and ask the tailor to copy it.

You may hear

我能帮你吗?	*wǒ néng bāng nǐ ma?*	Can I help you?
有人帮你吗?	*yǒu rén bāng nǐ ma?*	Have you been served?
什么号?	*shén me hào?*	What size?
我们没有	*wǒ men méi yǒu*	We don't have any
就这个	*jiù zhè ge*	Here you are
还要别的吗?	*hái yào bié de ma?*	Anything else?
我能把它打包给你吗?	*wǒ néng bǎ tā tǎ bāo gěi nǐ ma?*	Shall I wrap it for you?

| 是（五十）元 | shì (wǔ shí) yuán | It's (50) yuan |
| 已经打折了 | yǐ jīng dǎ zhé le | It's reduced |

Quality control
Whatever you buy, check it yourself to ensure it's of decent quality. Seams on clothes should be well-hemmed and there should be no puckering. With jewellery and accessories, make sure that the fastenings and zips work.

Where to shop

Where can I find a...	...在哪里?	...zài nǎ lǐ?
- bookshop?	- 书店	- shū diàn
- clothes shop?	- 服装店	- fú zhuāng diàn
- department store?	- 百货商店	- bǎi huò shāng diàn
- gift shop?	- 礼品店	- lǐ pǐn diàn
- music shop?	- 音乐商店	- yīn yuè shāng diàn
- market?	- 市场	- shì chǎng
- newsagent?	- 报摊	- bào tān
- shoe shop?	- 鞋店	- xié diàn
- stationer's?	- 文具店	- wén jù diàn
- tobacconist?	- 烟草店	- yān cǎo diàn
- souvenir shop?	- 纪念品店	- jì niàn pǐn diàn

Where's the best place to buy...?	卖...的好商店在哪里?	mài... de hǎo shāng diàn zài nǎ li?
- a camera film	- 照相机影片	- zhào xiàng jī yǐng piàn
- an English newspaper	- 英文报纸	- yīng wén bào zhǐ
- a map	- 地图	- dì tú
- postcards	- 明信片	- míng xìn piàn
- a present	- 礼品	- lǐ pǐn
- stamps	- 邮票	- yóu piào
- sun cream	- 防晒霜	- fáng shài shuāng

Food & markets

| Is there a supermarket/ market nearby? | 附近有超级市场/ 食品市场吗? | *fù jìn yǒu chāo jí shì chǎng/shí pǐn shì chǎng ma?* |

Can I have... | 请给我... | *qǐng gěi wǒ...*
- some bread? | – 面包 | *- miàn bāo*
- some fruit? | – 水果 | *- shuǐ guǒ*
- some cheese? | – 乳酪 | *- rǔ lào*
- a bottle of water? | – 一瓶水 | *- yì píng shuǐ*
- a bottle of wine? | – 一瓶葡萄酒 | *- yì píng pú táo jiǔ*

I'd like... of that | 请给我... | *qǐng gěi wǒ...*
- half a kilo | – 半公斤 | *- bàn gōng jīn*
- 250 grams | – 两百五十克 | *- liǎng bǎi wǔ shí kè*
- a small/big piece | – 一小/大块 | *- yí xiǎo/dà kuài*

Import & export

If you're buying furniture or other large items that need to be shipped back to the UK, the merchant should take care of all the necessary paperwork for you, including informing you of any customs duties that may be imposed on exports. If they refuse to do this, this should ring alarm bells about the degree of zeal with which they stick to legal requirements, and you would be very wise not to make the purchase. Note that there are restrictions on exporting antiques: once again, the vendor should be able to advise you. There is as yet no system for reclaiming tax on purchases made in China.

Too good to be true
It's still really easy to find fake luxury goods all over China. Items range from the obviously fake – like T-shirts with the Chanel logo emblazoned across the chest – to some very realistic imitations.

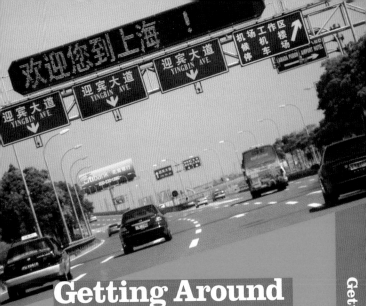

Getting Around

Getting Around

Visitors can choose between the vast rail network or plentiful bus routes to hop between cities and towns. Rail travel is cheap and comfortable, and there are also long-distance buses to almost every small town in the country. However, roads are often non-existent if you're far from the main cities, so the journey is likely to be bumpy. Flying is still the quickest way to get between cities.

You may want to rent a car, but cross-country driving isn't recommended because of the sheer distances and poor roads. There's also not that much to see along the way.

37

Arrival

There are international airports in the main cities, including Beijing, Shanghai, Xi'an, Chongqing, Tianjin, Guangzhou and Shenzhen. These are all served by flights from the UK. Shenzhen is also a common overland entry point, as it borders Hong Kong with trains arriving almost every hour. British passport holders must have a valid visa that has been issued before arrival.

Where is/are the...	...在哪里?	... zài nǎ li?
- luggage from flight...?	– 从航班... 的行李	- cóng háng bān... de xíng li
- luggage trolleys?	– 手推车	- shǒu tuī chē
- lost luggage office?	– 行李查询中心	- xíng lǐ chá xún zhōng xīn

Where is/are the...	...在哪里?	... zài nǎ lǐ?
- buses?	– 公共汽车	- gōng gòng qì chē
- trains?	– 火车	- huǒ chē
- taxis?	– 出租车	- chū zū chē
- car rental?	– 租车	- zū chē
- exit?	– 出口	- chū kǒu

How do I get to hotel...?	我怎么去... 旅馆?	wǒ zěn me qù... lǔ guǎn?

My baggage is...	我的行李...	wǒ de xíng li...
- lost	– 丢了	- diū le
- damaged	– 损坏了	- sǔn huài le
- stolen	– 被偷了	- bèi tōu le

Taken for a ride

If you're not being met at the airport, chances are that as you enter the arrivals area, you'll be accosted by taxi touts. Reject them for the taxi queue, which should be just outside the terminal, where you'll find metered cabs.

Ride and park
Although many Chinese are shunning cycling in favour of gas-guzzling cars, it's still a popular method of transportation, especially in smaller cities. Bikes can be rented from hotels, bicycle shops or kiosks around town.

Customs
You will be required to fill in a declaration form listing any valuables you are carrying. Apart from gifts, all the items on the form must be taken with you when you leave. In addition to the items usually prohibited by customs authorities around the world, China does not admit fresh fruit and pornographic or anti-government material.

The children are on this passport	孩子们使用这本护照	hái zi mén shǐ yòng zhè běn hù zhào
We're here on holiday	我们在度假	wǒ men zài dù jià
I'm going to...	我要去...	wǒ yào qù...
I have nothing to declare	我不需要申报	wǒ bù xū yào shēn bào
Do I have to declare this?	我需要申报这个吗?	wǒ xū yào shēn bào zhè ge ma?

Car hire
Local and international rental car companies operate only in major cities, with cars mainly for driving within city limits. And unless you have a local driving licence, the car will come with a driver. It is, however, possible to find inter-city hire companies.

I'd like to hire a...	我想租...	wǒ xiǎng zū...
- car	– 一辆汽车	- yí liàng qì chē
- people carrier	– 一辆微型货车	- yí liàng wēi xíng huò chē
with...	带...	dài...
- air conditioning	– 空调	- kōng tiáo

- automatic transmission	– 自动变速	- *zì dòng biàn sù*
How much is that for a...	...多少钱?	*... duō shǎo qián?*
- day?	– 每天	- *měi tiān*
- week?	– 每星期	- *měi xīng qī*
Does that include...	包括...吗?	*bāo kuò... ma?*
- mileage?	– 里程	- *lǐ chéng*
- insurance?	– 保险	- *bǎo xiǎn*

On the road

As a relatively new economy, the number of cars on Chinese roads has gone up at a much greater rate than the number of competent drivers. Expect haphazard driving, with little attention paid to etiquette, traffic lights or road signs.

What is the speed limit?	限速是什么?	*xiàn sù shì shén me?*
Can I park here?	我可以停在这里吗?	*wǒ kě yǐ tíng zài zhè li ma?*
Where is a petrol station?	加油站在哪里?	*jiā yóu zhàn zài nǎ li?*
Please fill up the tank with...	请加满...	*qǐng jiā mǎn...*
- unleaded	– 无铅汽油	- *wú qiān qì yóu*
- diesel	– 柴油	- *chái yóu*
- leaded	– 有铅汽油	- *yǒu qiān qì yóu*
- LPG	– 液化石油汽	- *yè huà shí yóu qì*

Directions

Is this the road to...?	这是去...的路吗?	*zhè shì qù... de lù ma?*
How do I get to...?	怎么去...?	*zén me qù...?*
How far is it to...?	...有多远?	*... yǒu duō yuǎn?*
How long will it take to...?	去... 多长时间?	*qù... duō cháng shí jiān?*
Could you point it out on the map?	你能在地图上指给我看吗?	*nǐ néng zài dì tū shàng zhǐ gěi wǒ kàn ma?*
I've lost my way	我迷路了	*wǒ mí lù le*
On the right/left	在右/左边	*zài yòu/zuǒ biān*
Turn right/left	右/左转	*yòu/zuǒ zhuǎn*
Straight ahead	一直走	*yì zhí zǒu*
Turn around	回头	*huí tóu*

All aboard!
Choose from three different types of train service: express (*kuài chē*, 快车), regular (*màn chē*, 慢车) and direct (*zhí dá*, 直达). There are five classes of seats: hard seat, soft seat, hard sleeper, soft sleeper and standing.

Public transport

Public transport is cheap and reliable. Large cities have easy-to-use underground systems; in smaller towns, your best bet will be to take public buses or to rent a bicycle. The inter-city rail network is extensive and very punctual.

Bus	公共汽车	*gōng gòng qì chē*
Bus station	公共汽车站	*gōng gòng qì chē zhàn*
Train	火车	*huǒ chē*
Train station	火车站	*huǒ chē zhàn*
I would like to go to...	我想去...	*wǒ xiǎng qù...*
I would like a... ticket	我要一张... 票	*wǒ yào yì zhāng... piào*
- single	– 单程	- *dān chéng*
- return	– 双程	- *shuāng chéng*
- first class	– 头等舱	- *tóu děng cāng*
- smoking/ non-smoking	– 吸烟/禁烟	- *xī yān/jìn yān*
What time does it leave/arrive?	几点离开/到达	*jǐ diǎn lí kāi/dào dá*
Could you tell me when to get off?	你能告诉我什么时候下车吗?	*ní néng gào sù wǒ shén me shí hòu xià chē ma?*

Taxis

In the bigger cities, taxis are plentiful and easily flagged down. All are metered, although drivers, particularly in small towns, might try to negotiate a flat fee. If this happens, ask them to turn the meter on, or simply get another cab.

I'd like a taxi to...	我想叫出租车去...	*wǒ xiǎng jiào chū zū chē qù...*
How much is it to the...	去... 要多少钱?	*qù... yào duō shǎo qián?*
- airport?	– 机场	*- jī chǎng*
- town centre?	– 市中心	*- shì zhōng xīn*
- hotel?	– 旅馆?	*- lǚ guǎn?*

Tours

You haven't seen China until you've seen the Great Wall. Nothing can prepare you for the scale of its magnificence. There is no shortage of day trips, so prepare to be awed.

Are there any organised tours of the town/region?	有城市/区域的旅行团吗?	*yǒu chéng shì/qū yù de lǚ xíng tuán ma?*
Where do they leave from?	旅行团从哪里出发?	*lǚ xíng tuán cóng nǎ li chū fā?*
What time does it start?	什么时候开始?	*shén me shí hòu kāi shǐ?*
Do you have English-speaking guides?	有说英语的导游吗?	*yǒu shuō yīng yǔ de dǎo yóu ma?*
Is lunch/tea included?	包括午餐/下午茶吗?	*bāo kuò wǔ cān/xià wǔ chá ma?*
Do we get any free time?	我们会有自由时间吗?	*wǒ men huì yǒu zì yóu shí jiān ma?*
Are we going to see...?	我们会看看... 吗?	*wǒ men huì kàn kan... ma?*
What time do we get back?	我们什么时候回来?	*wǒ men shén me shí hòu huí lái?*

Getting into gear

In addition to public buses for general city transportation, you will also find tourist buses, which specialise in sightseeing tours, and inter-city buses for long distance travel. Ask your hotel for information.

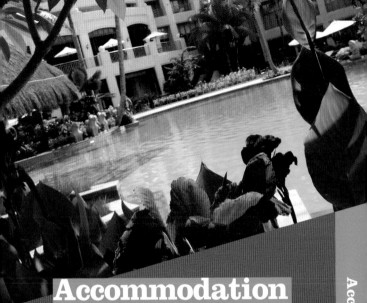

Accommodation

There's a huge choice of accommodation, from guest houses to top-tier hotels. Youth hostels are a good option if you're travelling on a shoestring. One step up from these are guest houses, which are private homes where families let rooms out. B&Bs are another popular choice. Most of the luxury hotels belong to international chains, and a number of boutique hotels are popping up in the larger cities.

It's best to reserve accommodation in advance, particularly if you're travelling during the main tourist seasons of May, September and October.

Types of accommodation

Hotels in China, even international chains, tend to be less expensive than in the UK. If you are planning to check in after 6pm, make sure you inform the accommodation in advance, particularly if it's a hostel or guest house. It is generally okay for unmarried couples to share a room, although some eyebrows might be raised if you're a foreign guy travelling with a local girl.

I'd like to stay in...	我想在... 住	wǒ xiǎng zài... zhù
- an apartment	- 公寓	- gōng yù
- a campsite	- 露营地	- lù yíng dì
- a hotel	- 旅馆	- lǚ guǎn
- a serviced room	- 服务室	- fú wù shì
- a youth hostel	- 青年旅社	- qīng nián lǚ shè
- a guest house	- 宾馆	- bīn guǎn

Is it...	是... 吗?	shì... ma?
- full board?	- 包括每顿饭餐	- bāo kuò měi dùn fàn cān
- half board?	- 包括早餐和别的饭餐	- bāo kuò zǎo cān hé bié de fàn cān
- self-catering?	- 自己承办酒席	- zì jǐ chéng bàn jiǔ xí

Reservations

Do you have any rooms available?	有可用的房间吗?	yǒu kě yòng de fáng jiān ma?
Can you recommend anywhere else?	你能推荐别的地方吗?	nǐ néng tuī jiàn bié de dì fāng ma?

Stars in their eyes

In theory, the China Tourist Hotel Star Rating Committee classifies accommodation from 1- to 5-star. In practice, however, there's no real enforcement of criteria and only 4- and 5-star ratings (top-end hotels) can be relied upon to have any consistency of service and quality.

I'd like to make a reservation for...	我要预定住...	*wǒ yào yù dìng zhù...*
- tonight	- 今天晚上	- *jīn tiān wǎn shàng*
- one night	- 一晚	- *yì wǎn*
- two nights	- 两晚	- *liǎng wǎn*
- a week	- 一个星期	- *yí gè xīng qī*
From... (1st May) to... (8th May)	从... （五月一号）到... （五月八号）	*cóng... (wǔ yuè yī hào) dào... (wǔ yuè bā hào)*

Stepping back in time

Venture off the beaten track and stay in one of the increasing number of restored old houses with traditional courtyards, which may feature fish ponds, ancient trees and quaint stone paving. A little online diligence should help you find these timeless treasures.

Room types

Single rooms will have one single or a queen bed, and usually just enough floor space to walk about. Twin rooms are the same, with two beds instead of one. Double rooms accommodate two sharing a queen- or king-sized bed. Don't expect a TV, internet connection or en suite facilities unless you're at a 3-star facility or better.

Do you have a... room?	有... 的房间吗？	*yǒu... de fáng jián ma?*
- single	- 单人	- *dān rén*
- double	- 双人	- *shuāng rén*
- family	- 家庭	- *jiā tíng*
with...	带...	*dài...*
- a cot?	- 轻便小床	- *qīng biàn xiǎo chuáng*
- twin beds?	- 单人床	- *dān rén chuáng*
- a double bed?	- 双人床	- *shuāng rén chuáng*
- a bath/shower?	- 浴缸/淋浴	- *yù gāng/lín yù*

45

- air conditioning?	– 空调	- kōng tiáo
- Internet access?	– 联网服务	- lián wǎng fú wù
Can I see the room?	我能看看房间吗？	wǒ néng kàn kan fáng jiān ma?

Cash for kip
There are numerous hostels across China offering dormitory-style sleeping options. Private rooms, sleeping anywhere from one to six, are also available. Book in advance and bring cash to pay for your stay.

打請
擾勿
DON'T
TROUBLE PLEASE

Prices

When you book your accommodation, you may be asked if you want breakfast included. This is worth considering especially if you're staying at a decent hotel, as there is usually a buffet with Asian and Western options, with plenty to set you up for the rest of the day. Tipping is not expected, except if the porter takes your luggage to your room when you first arrive.

How much is...	... 多少钱？	... duō shǎo qián?
- a double room?	– 双人间	- shuāng rén jiān
- per night?	– 每晚	- měi wǎn
- per week?	– 每星期	- měi xīng qī
Is breakfast included?	包括早餐吗？	bāo kuò zǎo cān ma?
Do you have...	有... 吗？	yǒu... ma?
- a reduction for children?	– 孩子折扣	- hái zi zhé kòu
- a single room supplement?	– 单人额外费	- dān rén é wài fèi
Is there...	有... 吗？	yǒu... ma?
- a swimming pool?	– 游泳池	- yóu yǒng chí
- a lift?	– 电梯	- diàn tī

I'll take it	我要这个房间	*wǒ yào zhè ge fáng jiān*
Can I pay by...	能用... 付款吗?	*néng yòng... fù kuǎn ma?*
- credit card?	– 信用卡?	- *xìn yòng kǎ*
- traveller's cheque?	– 旅行支票	- *lǚ xíng zhī piào*

Special requests

Could you...	可以... 吗?	*kě yǐ... ma?*
- put this in the hotel safe?	– 把这个留在保险柜	- *bǎ zhè ge liú zài bǎo xiǎn guì*
- order a taxi for me?	– 给我叫一辆出租车	- *géi wǒ jiào yí liàng chū zū chē*
- wake me up at (7am)?	– 在(早晨七点)叫醒我	- *zài (zǎo chén qī diǎn) jiào xǐng wǒ*
Can I have a room with...	我能要一个...的房间吗?	*wǒ néng yào yí gè... de fáng jiān ma?*
- a sea view?	– 海景	- *hǎi jǐng*
- a bigger room?	– 更大	- *gèng dà*
- a quieter room?	– 更安静	- *gèng ān jìng*
Is there...	有... 吗?	*yǒu... ma?*
- a safe?	– 保险柜	- *bǎo xiǎn guì*
- a babysitting service?	– 保姆服务	- *bǎo mǔ fú wù*
- a laundry service?	– 洗衣服务	- *xǐ yī fú wù*
Is there wheelchair access?	有轮椅通道吗?	*yǒu lún yǐ tōng dào ma?*

Checking in & out

I have a reservation for tonight	我有住今晚的预定	*wǒ yǒu zhù jīn wǎn de yù dìng*
In the name of...	名义是...	*míng yì shì...*
Here's my passport	这是我的护照	*zhè shì wǒ de hù zhào*
What time is check out?	几点退房?	*jǐ diǎn tuì fáng?*
Can I have a later check out?	能迟一点退房吗?	*néng chí yì diǎn tuì fáng ma?*
Can I leave my bags here?	我可以把包留在这里吗?	*wǒ kě yǐ bǎ bāo liú zài zhè li ma?*

| I'd like to check out | 我想退房 | *wǒ xiǎng tuì fáng* |
| Can I have the bill? | 可以给我账单吗? | *kě yǐ gěi wǒ zhàng dān ma?* |

Camping

Do you have...	有... 吗?	*yǒu... ma?*
- a site available?	– 可用的露营地	- *kě yòng de lù yíng dì*
- electricity?	– 电	- *diàn*
- hot showers?	– 热水的淋浴	- *rè shuǐ de lín yù*
- tents for hire?	– 供出租的帐篷	- *gòng chū zū de zhàng peng*

How much is it per...	每... 多少钱?	*měi... duō shǎo qián?*
- tent?	– 帐篷	- *zhàng peng*
- caravan?	– 有篷卡车	- *yǒu péng kǎ chē*
- person?	– 人	- *rén*
- car?	– 车	- *chē*

Where is/are the...	... 在哪里?	*... zài ná li?*
- reception?	– 服务台	- *fú wù tái*
- bathrooms?	– 浴室	- *yù shì*
- laundry facilities?	– 洗衣服务	- *xǐ yī fú wù*

Out in the cold

Unlike the European mindset of camping as a fun activity, Chinese people do not see the point in "roughing it". As a result, camping is not common, although there are some sites located near nature reserves or other natural attractions.

Survival Guide

China may seem like a bewildering place; it isn't. Its banks, chemists, post offices and phones are much the same as the UK's.

There are ATMs aplenty, but not all of them accept foreign cards. If you're exchanging money, hold on to the receipts so you can convert back into foreign currency when you leave.

Although the situation is improving, China is not an easy place for travellers with disabilities. Make sure that you inform your travel agent and hotel as early as possible so that they can make any necessary arrangements.

Money & banks

Where is the nearest...	（最近的）... 在哪里?	(zuì jìn de)... zài nǎ li?
- bank?	- 银行	- yín háng
- ATM/bank machine?	- 自动取款机	- zì dòng qǔ kuǎn jī
- foreign exchange office?	- 货币兑换处	- huò bì duì huàn chù

I'd like to...	我想...	wǒ xiǎng...
- withdraw money	- 取钱	- qǔ qián
- cash a traveller's cheque	- 把旅行支票换成现金	- bǎ lǚ xíng zhī piào huàn chéng xiàn jīn
- change money	- 换钱	- huàn qián
- arrange a transfer	- 转账	- zhuǎn zhàng

Could I have smaller notes, please?	能换成小面值纸币吗?	néng huàn chéng xiǎo miàn zhí zhǐ bì ma?
What's the exchange rate?	外币兑换率是多少?	wài bì duì huàn lǜ shì duō shǎo?
What's the commission?	手续费是多少?	shǒu xù fèi shi duō shǎo?
What's the charge for...	... 费用是多少?	... fèi yòng shì duō shǎo?
- making a withdrawal?	- 撤出金钱	- chè chū jīn qián
- exchanging money?	- 兑换钱	- duì huàn qián

Show me the money

If you're planning to withdraw money from a bank machine, head for a Bank of China or Industrial and Commercial Bank of China ATM, as these accept foreign cards. There are also HSBC and Citibank machines, but these are few and far between.

- cashing a cheque?	- 兑现支票	- duì xiàn zhī piào
What's the minimum/ maximum amount?	最大值/极小值是多少?	zuì dà zhí/jí xiǎo zhí shì duō shǎo?
This is not right	出错了	chū cuò le
Is there a problem with my account?	我的账户有问题吗?	wǒ de zhàng hù yǒu wèn tí ma?
The ATM/bank machine took my card	自动取款机吞了我的信用卡	zì dòng qǔ kuǎn jī tūn le wǒ de xìn yòng kǎ
I've forgotten my PIN	我忘记了我的密码	wǒ wàng jì le wǒ de mì mǎ

Post office

Where is the (main) post office?	(主要)邮局在哪里?	(zhǔ yào) yóu jú zài ná lǐ?
I'd like to send a...	我想...	wǒ xiǎng...
- letter	- 寄信	- jì xìn
- postcard	- 寄明信片	- jì míng xìn piàn
- parcel	- 寄包裹	- jì bāo guǒ
- fax	- 发传真	- fā chuán zhēn
I'd like to send this...	我要...	wǒ yào...
- to the United Kingdom	- 把它寄到英国去	- bǎ tā jì dào yīng guó qù
- by airmail	- 用航空	- yòng háng kōng
- by express mail	- 用快件	- yòng kuài jiàn
- by registered mail	- 发挂号信	- fā guà hào xìn
I'd like...	我要...	wǒ yào...
- a stamp for this letter/postcard	- 买这封信/这张明信片的邮票	- mǎi zhè fēng xìn/zhè zhāng míng xìn piàn de yóu piào
- to buy envelopes	- 买信封	- mǎi xìn fēng
- to make a photocopy	- 复印	- fù yìn
It contains...	里面装的是...	lǐ miàn zhuāng de shì...
It's fragile	是易碎的	shì yì suì de

51

Telecoms

Where can I make an international phone call?	哪里能打国际电话?	*nǎ li néng dǎ guó jì diàn huà?*
Where can I buy a phone card?	哪里能买电话卡?	*nǎ li néng mǎi diàn huà kǎ?*
How do I call abroad?	我怎么打国际电话?	*wǒ zén me dǎ guó jì diàn huà?*
How much does it cost per minute?	每分钟多少钱?	*měi fēn zhōng duō shǎo qián?*
The number is...	电话号码是...	*diàn huà hào mǎ shì...*
What's the area/ country code for...?	... 的区号/ 国家代码是什么?	*... de qū hào/guó jiā dài mǎ shì shén me?*
The number is engaged	号码不能连接	*hào mǎ bù néng lián jiē*
The connection is bad	连接不好	*lián jiē bù hǎo*
I've been cut off	我被挂断了	*wǒ bèi guà duàn le*
I'd like...	我需要...	*wǒ xū yào...*
- a charger for my mobile phone	- 移动电话充电器	*- yí dòng diàn huà chōng diàn qì*
- an adaptor plug	- 变压器	*- biàn yā qì*
- a pre-paid SIM card	- 预付用户标识模块/ SIM 卡	*- yù fù yòng hù biāo zhì mó kuài/ SIM kǎ*

Internet

Where's the nearest Internet café?	最近的网吧在哪里?	*zuì jìn de wǎng bā zài nǎ li?*
Can I access the Internet here?	我能上网吗?	*wǒ néng shàng wǎng ma?*
I'd like to...	我想...	*wǒ xiǎng...*
- use the Internet	- 上网	*- shàng wǎng*
- check my email	- 查电子邮件	*- chá diàn zǐ yóu jiàn*
- use a printer	- 打印	*- dǎ yìn*
How much is it...	...多少钱?	*...duō shǎo qián?*
- per minute?	- 每分钟	*- měi fēn zhōng*
- per hour?	- 每小时	*- měi xiǎo shí*
- to buy a CD?	- 买光盘	*- mǎi guāng pán*

How do I...	怎么...	*zén me...*
- log on?	– 登录	*- dēng lù*
- open a browser?	– 上网	*- shàng wǎng*
- print this?	– 打印	*- dǎ yìn*
I need help with this computer	我需要帮助	*wǒ xū yào bāng zhù*
The computer has crashed	电脑坏了	*diàn nǎo huài le*
I've finished	用完了	*yòng wán le*

Surf's up
There are lots of Internet cafés in China, and they're cheap. Known as *wǎng bā* (网吧), they are required by law to have cameras installed that record the identity of their patrons, who must be 18 or over.

Chemist

Where's the nearest (all-night) pharmacy?	最近的(二十四小时)药房在哪里?	*zuì jìn de (èr shí sì xiǎo shí) yào fáng zài nǎ li?*
What time does the pharmacy open/close?	药房什么时候开门/关门?	*yào fáng shén me shí hou kāi mén/guān mén?*
I need something for...	我需要治... 的药	*wǒ xū yào zhì... de yào*
- diarrhoea	– 腹泻	*- fù xiè*
- a cold	– 感冒	*- gǎn mào*
- a cough	– 咳嗽	*- ké sou*
- insect bites	– 虫咬	*- chóng yǎo*
- sunburn	– 晒伤	*- shài shāng*
- motion sickness	– 运动病	*- yùn dòng bìng*
- hay fever	– 花粉症	*- huā fěn zhèng*
- period pain	– 经期腹痛	*- jīng qī fù tòng*

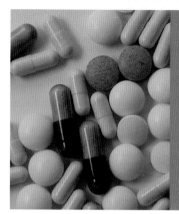

Fighting fit

Chemists are generally open from 9am to 9pm. The larger cities will have some 24-hour chemists. In an emergency, go to the nearest hospital or ask if there's an international medical centre that has round-the-clock services.

- abdominal pains	- 胃肠痛	- wěi cháng tòng
- a urine infection	- 膀胱感染	- páng guāng gǎn rǎn
- a vaginal infection	- 阴道感染	- yīn dào gǎn rǎn
I'd like...	我要...	wǒ yào...
- aspirin	- 阿斯匹林	- ā sī pī lín
- plasters	- 膏药	- gāo yào
- condoms	- 避孕套	- bì yùn tào
- insect repellent	- 杀虫剂	- shā chóng jì
- painkillers	- 镇痛药	- zhèn tòng yào
- a contraceptive	- 避孕药	- bì yùn yào
How much should I take?	我吃多少呢?	wǒ chī duō shǎo ne?
Take...	吃...	chī...
- a tablet	- 一片剂	- yí piàn jì
- a teaspoon	- 一茶匙	- yì chá chí
Take with water	和水吃	hé shuǐ chī
How often should I take this?	多长时间吃一次?	duō cháng shí jiān chī yí cì?
- once/twice a day	- 一天一次/两次	- yì tiān yí cì/liǎng cì
- before/after meals	- 饭前/饭后	- fàn qián/fàn hòu
- in the morning/ evening	- 上午/晚上	- shàng wǔ/ wǎn shàng
Is it suitable for children?	对孩子安全吗?	duì hái zi ān quán ma?

Will it make me drowsy?	可能使人发困吗?	kě néng shǐ rén fā kùn ma?
Do I need a prescription?	需要处方吗?	xū yào chǔ fāng ma?
I have a prescription	我有处方	wǒ yǒu chǔ fāng

Children

Where should I take the children?	你能推荐孩子玩的地方吗?	nǐ néng tuī jiàn hái zi wán de dì fāng ma?
Where is the nearest...	最近的... 在哪里?	zuì jìn de... zài nǎ li?
- playground?	– 操场	- cāo chǎng
- fairground?	– 游乐园	- yóu lè yuán
- zoo?	– 动物园	- dòng wù yuán
- park?	– 公园	- gōng yuán
- swimming pool?	– 游泳池	- yóu yǒng chí
Is this suitable for children?	它适合孩子吗?	tā shì hé hái zi ma?
Are children allowed?	孩子可以进去吗?	hái zi kě yǐ jìn qù ma?
Are there baby-changing facilities here?	有给孩子换尿布的设施吗?	yǒu gěi hái zi huàn niào bù de shè shī ma?
Do you have...	你有... 吗?	nǐ yǒu... ma?
- a children's menu?	– 儿童菜单	- ér tong cài dān
- a high chair?	– 高脚椅	- gāo jiǎo yǐ
Is there...	有... 吗?	yǒu... ma?
- a child-minding service?	– 保姆	- bǎo mǔ
- a nursery?	– 托儿所	- tuō er suǒ
Can you recommend a reliable babysitter?	你能推荐一位可靠的保姆吗?	nǐ néng tuī jiàn yí wèi kě kào de bǎo mǔ ma?
Are the children constantly supervised?	孩子们总是被监督吗?	hái zi mén zǒng shì bèi jiān dū ma?

When can I bring them?	我什么时候能带他们来？	*wǒ shén me shí hòu néng dài tā mén lái?*
What time do I have to pick them up?	我什么时候需要接他们？	*wǒ shén me shí hòu xū yào jiē tā mén?*
He/she is ... years old	他/她... 岁	*tā/tā... suì*
I'd like to buy...	我想买...	*wǒ xiǎng mǎi...*
- nappies	- 尿布湿	*- niào bù shī*
- baby wipes	- 婴儿食品	*- yīng ér shí pǐn*
- tissues	- 面巾纸	*- miàn jīn zhǐ*

Travellers with disabilities

I have a disability	我是残疾人	*wǒ shì cán jí rén*
I need assistance	我需要帮助	*wǒ xū yào bāng zhù*
I am blind	我是瞎的	*wǒ shì xiā de*
I am deaf	我耳聋	*wǒ ěr lóng*
I have a hearing aid	我有助听机	*wǒ yǒu zhù tīng jī*
I can't walk well	我不能走远路	*wǒ bù néng zǒu yuǎn lù*
Is there a lift?	有电梯吗？	*yǒu diàn tī ma?*
Is there wheelchair access?	有轮椅通道吗？	*yǒu lún yǐ tōng dào ma?*
Can I bring my guide dog?	允许导盲犬吗？	*yǔn xǔ dǎo máng quǎn ma?*
Are there disabled toilets?	有残疾人用的洗手间吗？	*yǒu cán jí rén yòng de xǐ shǒu jiān ma?*
Do you offer disabled services?	你有残疾服务吗？	*nǐ yǒu cán jí fú wù ma?*
Could you help me...	你能帮我... 吗？	*nǐ néng bāng wǒ... ma?*
- cross the street?	- 过马路	*- guò mǎ lù*
- go up/down the stairs?	- 上楼/下楼	*- shàng lóu/xià lóu*
Can I sit down somewhere?	我可以坐下吗？	*wǒ kě yǐ zuò xià ma?*
Could you call an accessible taxi for me?	你能帮我叫一辆残疾人出租车吗？	*nǐ néng bāng wǒ jiào yī liàng cán jí rén chū zū chē ma?*

Repairs & cleaning

This is broken	这坏了	*zhè huài le*
Can you fix it?	你能修吗?	*nǐ néng xiū ma?*
Do you have...	你有... 吗?	*nǐ yǒu... ma?*
- a battery?	– 电池	*- diàn chí*
- spare parts?	– 备件	*- bèi jiàn*
Can you ... this?	你能... 这条衣吗?	*nǐ néng... zhè tiáo yī ma?*
- clean	– 清洗	*- qīng xǐ*
- press	– 熨	*- yùn*
- dry clean	– 干洗	*- gān xǐ*
- patch	– 补	*- bǔ*
When will it be ready?	什么时候能做好?	*shén me shí hòu néng zuò hǎo?*
This isn't mine	这不是我的	*zhè bú shì wǒ de*

A good call

Now that mobile phones have taken off in China, public phones are scarce. Make sure you have enough change as the ones that do remain are usually coin operated.

Tourist information

Where's the Tourist Information Office?	旅游信息办公室在哪里?	*lǚ yóu xìn xī bàn gōng shì zài nǎ li?*
Do you have a city/ regional map?	你有城市/区域的地图吗?	*nǐ yǒu chéng shì/qū yù de dì tú ma?*
What are the main places of interest?	主要景点是什么?	*zhǔ yào jǐng diǎn shì shén me?*
Could you show me on the map?	你能在地图上指给我看吗?	*nǐ néng zài dì tú shàng zhǐ gěi wǒ kàn ma?*
We'll be here for...	我们在这里...	*wǒ mén zài zhè li...*
- half a day	– 半天	*- bàn tiān*
- a day	– 一天	*- yì tiān*
- a week	– 一个星期	*- yí gè xīng qī*

Do you have a brochure in English?	有英语的旅游手册吗?	*yǒu yīng yǔ de lǚ yóu shǒu cè ma?*
We're interested in...	我们的兴趣是...	*wǒ men de xìng qù shì...*
- history	– 历史	*- lì shǐ*
- architecture	– 建筑学	*- jiàn zhù xué*
- shopping	– 购物	*- gòu wù*
- hiking	– 远足	*- yuǎn zú*
- a scenic walk	– 风景步行	*- fēng jǐng bù xíng*
- a boat cruise	– 小船巡航	*- xiǎo chuán xún háng*
- a guided tour	– 游览	*- yóu lǎn*
Are there any excursions?	有游览吗?	*yǒu yóu lǎn ma?*
How long does it take?	需要多久?	*xū yào duō jiǔ?*
What does it cost?	多少钱?	*duō shǎo qián?*
What days is it open/closed?	哪天开门/关门?	*nǎ tiān kāi mén/ guān mén?*
What time does it open/close?	几点开门/关门?	*jǐ diǎn kāi mén/ guān mén?*
What's the admission price?	入场费是多少?	*rù chǎng fèi shì duō shǎo?*
Are there any tours in English?	有英语导游吗?	*yǒu yīng yǔ dǎo yóu ma?*

Home sweet home

To make an IDD call to the UK, dial 00 + 44 + area code + phone number. Cheaper rates can be had with international phone cards, which you can buy in grocery stores. There will be instructions on the back of the card on usage.

Emergencies

As part of your pre-visit preparations, do make sure that you arrange travel insurance that covers medical emergencies. If you're unfortunate enough to experience one, head to the nearest hospital A&E. You might be asked to make a deposit prior to admission to cover the expected cost of the treatment, so, if possible, try to have some money on you.

If you've been the victim of crime, report it immediately at the nearest police station, and take someone who can speak Mandarin along with you. The British Embassy can help with information about the local police procedures, but can't give legal advice.

Medical

Where is...	...在哪里?	...zài nǎ li?
- the hospital?	- 医院	- yī yuàn
- the health centre?	- 诊所	- zhěn suǒ
I need...	我需要...	wǒ xū yào...
- a doctor	- 医生	- yī shēng
- a female doctor	- 女性医生	- nǚ xìng yī shēng
- an ambulance	- 救护车	- jiù hù chē
It's very urgent	很急	hěn jí
I'm injured	我受伤了	wǒ shòu shāng le
Can I see a doctor?	我能看医生吗?	wǒ néng kàn yī shēng ma?
I don't feel well	我病了	wǒ bìng le
I have...	我...	wǒ...
- a cold	- 得感冒	- dé gǎn mào
- diarrhoea	- 腹泻	- fù xiè
- a rash	- 出疹子了	- chū zhěn zi le
- a temperature	- 发烧	- fā shāo
I have a lump here	我有浮肿	wǒ yǒu fú zhǒng
It hurts here	这里疼	zhè li téng
It hurts a lot/a little	很疼/一点疼	hěn téng/ yì diǎn téng
How much do I owe you?	多少钱?	duō shǎo qián?
I have insurance	我有保险	wǒ yǒu bǎo xiǎn

Dentist

I need a dentist	我需要牙医	wǒ xū yào yá yī
I have tooth ache	我牙疼	wǒ yá téng
My gums are swollen	我有牙龈炎	wǒ yǒu yá yín yán
This filling has fallen out	我的补牙填料掉了	wǒ de bǔ yá tián liào diào le
I have an abscess	我的牙被感染了	wǒ de yá bèi gǎn rǎn le
I have broken a tooth	我有一颗断牙	wǒ yǒu yì kē duàn yá
Are you going to take it out?	你会把它去除吗?	nǐ huì bǎ tā qù chú ma?
Can you fix it temporarily?	你能临时修补吗?	nǐ néng lín shí xiū bǔ ma?

Crime

I want to report a theft	我想报告一次偷窃事件	*wǒ xiǎng bào gào yí cì tōu qiè shì jiàn*
Someone has stolen my...	我的... 被偷了	*wǒ de... bèi tōu le*
- bag	- 提包	- *tí bāo*
- car	- 汽车	- *qì chē*
- credit cards	- 信用卡	- *xìn yòng kǎ*
- money	- 钱	- *qián*
- passport	- 护照	- *hù zhào*
I've been attacked	我被攻击了	*wǒ bèi gōng jī le*

Lost property

I've lost my...	我的... 丢了	*wǒ de... diū le*
- car keys	- 汽车钥匙	- *qì chē yào shi*
- driving licence	- 驾照	- *jià zhào*
- handbag	- 提包	- *tí bāo*
- flight tickets	- 机票	- *jī piào*
It happened...	... 发生	*... fā shēng*
- this morning	- 今晨	- *jīn chén*
- today	- 今天	- *jīn tiān*
- in the hotel	- 在旅馆	- *zài lǚ guǎn*
I left it in the taxi	在出租车丢了	*zài chū zū chē diū le*

Breakdown

I've had...	我...	*wǒ...*
- an accident	- 出事故了	- *chū shì gù le*

- a breakdown	– 的汽车坏了	- de qì chē huài le
- a puncture	– 的轮胎泄了气	- de lún tāi xiè le qì
My battery is flat	电池用完了	diàn chí yòng wán le
I don't have a spare tyre	我没有备用轮胎	wǒ méi yǒu bèi yòng lún tāi
I've run out of petrol	汽油用完了	qì yóu yòng wán le
My car won't start	我的汽车不启动	wǒ de qì chē bú qǐ dòng
Can you repair it?	你能修好吗?	nǐ néng xiū hǎo ma?
How long will it take?	需要多久?	xū yào duō jiǔ?
I have breakdown cover	我有保险	wǒ yǒu bǎo xiǎn

Banish that bribe

If you've been stopped by the police, arrested or detained, you might be tempted to bribe your way out of trouble. Don't. Just be polite and cooperative. If the situation looks serious, contact the British Embassy for advice.

Problems with the authorities

I'm sorry, I didn't realise...	对不起，我没体会...	duì bu qǐ, wǒ méi tǐ huì...
- I was driving so fast	– 我驾得那么快	- wǒ jià de nà me kuài
- I went over the red lights	– 我闯了红灯	- wǒ chuǎng le hóng dēng
- it was against the law	– 这是非法的	- zhè shì fēi fǎ de
Here are my documents	这是我的文件	zhè shì wǒ de wén jiàn
I'm innocent	我是无辜的	wǒ shì wú gū de

Dictionary

This section consists of two parts: an English-Mandarin dictionary to help you get your point across and a Mandarin-English one to decipher the reply. In the Mandarin, we list the pinyin version first for easier reference. Characters that you are likely to see on signs are highlighted in magenta.

Don't forget that even if you feel a bit shy about sallying forth with the spoken language, the locals will love you just for trying... and if all else fails, you can always find a friendly face, smile in an appropriately winsome manner and simply point at the terms you need!

A

A&E	急症室	*jí zhèng shì*
a(n)	一个	*yí gè*
about (concerning)	关于	*guān yú*
accident	事故	*shì gù*
accommodation	住宿	*zhù sù*
aeroplane	飞机	*fēi jī*
again	再	*zài*
ago	以前	*yǐ qián*
AIDS	艾滋病	*ài zī bìng*
airmail	航空信	*háng kōng xìn*
airport	飞机场	*fēi jī chǎng*
alarm	警钟	*jǐng zhōng*
all	全部	*quán bù*
all right	行/ 好了	*xíng/hǎo le*
allergy	过敏	*guò mǐn*
ambulance	救护车	*jiù hù chē*

America	美国	*měi guó*

This word literally translates as "beautiful land". The most common explanation for this is that "America" used to be translated phonetically as *yà měi lì jiā* (亚美利加).

American	美国人	*měi guó rén*
and	和	*hé*
anniversary	周年纪念	*zhōu nián jì niàn*
another	别的	*bié de*
to answer	回答	*huí dá*
any	任何	*rèn hé*
apartment	公寓	*gōng yù*
appointment	约会	*yuē huì*
April	四月	*sì yuè*
area	区	*qū*
area code	区号	*qū hào*
around	在附近	*zài fù jìn*
to arrange	安排	*ān pái*
arrival	抵达	*dǐ dá*
art	艺术	*yì shù*
to ask	问	*wèn*
aspirin	阿司匹林	*ā sī pī lín*
at (time)	在	*zài*
August	八月	*bā yuè*
Australia	澳洲	*ào zhōu*
Australian	澳洲人	*ào zhōu rén*
available	可利用	*kě lì yòng*
away	离开	*lí kāi*

B

baby	婴孩	yīng hái
back (body)	背部	bèi bù
back (place)	后面	hòu miàn
bad	不好	bù hǎo
baggage	行李	xíng li

bar (pub) 酒吧 *jiǔ bā*

The bar scene has burgeoned in the last decade, driven both by foreign tourism and affluent young locals looking for a way to cut loose. Each major city has its own vibe.

bath	浴缸	yù gāng
to be	是	shì
beach	海滩	hǎi tān
because	因为	yīn wèi
because of	由于	yóu yú
best	最好	zuì hǎo
better	更好	gèng hǎo
between	在之间	zài zhī jiān
bicycle	自行车	zì xíng chē
big	大	dà
bill	账单	zhàng dān
bit (a)	一点	yì diǎn
boarding card	登机牌	dēng jī pái
book	书	shū
to book/booking	预定	yù dìng
box office	票房	piào fáng
boy	男孩	nán hái
brother	兄弟	xiōng dì
bureau de change	货币兑换处	huò bì duì huàn chù
to burn	烧	shāo
bus	公共汽车	gōng gòng qì chē
business	商务	shāng wù
but	可是	kě shì
to buy	买	mǎi
by (air, car, etc)	达	dá
by (beside)	在旁边	zài páng biān
by (via)	通过	tōng guò

C

café	小餐馆	xiǎo cān guǎn
to call	打电话	dǎ diàn huà
camera	照相机	zhào xiàng jī
can (to be able)	可以	ké yǐ
to cancel	取消	qǔ xiāo
car	车	chē

carnival	狂欢节	*kuáng huān jié*
cash	现金	*xiàn jīn*
cash point	自动取款机	*zì dòng qǔ kuǎn jī*
casino	赌博娱乐场	*dǔ bó yú lè chǎng*
cathedral	大教堂	*dà jiào táng*
CD	光盘/CD	*guāng pán/CD*
centre	中心	*zhōng xīn*
to change	换	*huàn*
charge	收费	*shōu fèi*
to charge	收费	*shōu fèi*
cheap	便宜	*pián yí*
to check in (hotel, airport)	办入住 (hotel); 办理登记手续 (airport)	*bàn rù zhù (hotel); bàn lǐ dēng jī shǒu xù (airport)*
cheque	支票	*zhī piào*
child	孩子	*hái zi*
to choose	选择	*xuǎn zé*
chopsticks	筷子	*kuài zi*
cigar	雪茄	*xuě jiā*
cigarette	香烟	*xiāng yān*
cinema	电影院	*diàn yǐng yuàn*
city	城市	*chéng shì*
to close	关门	*guān mén*
close by	靠近	*kào jìn*
closed	关闭	*guān bì*
clothes	衣物	*yī wù*
club	俱乐部	*jù lè bù*
coast	海岸	*hǎi àn*
coffee house	咖啡店	*kā fēi diàn*
cold	感冒 (illness); 冷 (temperature)	*gǎn mào (illness); lěng (temperature)*
colour	颜色	*yán sè*

to complain	**抱怨**	**bào yuàn**

You may have heard of *miàn zi* (面子), or "face". This is the impression you give in social interactions. In practice, this means that it's rude to embarrass someone, as both you and they "lose face".

complaint	怨言	*yuàn yán*
computer	电脑	*diàn nǎo*
to confirm	证实	*zhèng shí*
confirmation	确认	*què rèn*
consulate	领事馆	*lǐng shì guǎn*
to contact	联系	*lián xì*
contagious	传染	*chuán rǎn*
cool	凉	*liáng*
cost	收费	*shōu fèi*
to cost	花费	*huā fèi*

cot	轻便小床	qīng biàn xiǎo chuáng
country	国家	guó jiā
countryside	乡下	xiāng xià
cream	奶油	nǎi yóu
credit card	信用卡	xìn yòng kǎ
crime	罪行	zuì xíng
currency	货币	huò bì
customer	顾客	gù kè
customs	海关	hǎi guān
cut	伤口	shāng kǒu
to cut	剪	jiǎn
cycling	骑自行车	qí zì xíng chē

D

damage	损伤	sǔn shāng
danger	危险	wēi xiǎn
daughter	女孩子	nǚ hái zi
day	天	tiān
December	十二月	shí èr yuè
to dehydrate	脱水	tuō shuǐ
delay	晚点	wǎn diǎn
to dial	打电话	dǎ diàn huà
difficult	困难	kùn nán
directions	方向	fāng xiàng
dirty	肮脏	āng zāng
disabled	残疾	cán jí
discount	折扣	zhé kòu
district	区	qū
to disturb	干扰	gān rǎo

---

doctor 医生 *yī shēng*

Medical doctors here are well-qualified, although not necessarily trained in the sort of bedside charm that Brits might expect. Consultations tend to be abrupt and questions may not be entertained, as these are seen as challenging the doctor's authority.

---

double	双	shuāng
down	下	xià
to drive	开车	kāi chē
driver	司机	sī jī
driving licence	司机驾照	sī jī jià zhào
drug	毒	dú
to dry clean	干洗	gān xǐ
dry cleaner's	干洗店	gān xǐ diàn
during	期间	qī jiān
duty (tax)	关税	guān shuì

E

early	早	*zǎo*
e-mail	电子邮件	*diàn zǐ yóu jiàn*
embassy	使馆	*shǐ guǎn*
emergency	紧急状态	*jǐn jí zhuàng tài*
England	英国	*yīng guó*
English	英语 (language); 英国人 (person)	*yīng yǔ (language); yīng guó rén (person)*
enough	足够	*zú gòu*
entrance	入口	*rù kǒu*
error	差错	*chā cuò*
exactly	正确	*zhèng què*
exchange rate	兑换率	*duì huàn lǜ*
exhibition	陈列	*chén liè*
exit	出口	*chū kǒu*
express (delivery)	快递	*kuài dì*
express (train)	快车	*kuài chē*

F

facilities	设施	*shè shī*
far	远	*yuǎn*
father	父亲	*fù qīn*
favourite	最爱	*zuì ài*

| **February** | 二月 | *èr yuè* |

The Lunar Year falls either in early February or late January. The lead-up is frantic, with millions crisscrossing the country to get back to their families in time for the eve.

festivals	节日	*jié rì*
filling (station)	加油站	*jiā yóu zhàn*
film (camera)	胶卷	*jiāo juǎn*
film (cinema)	电影	*diàn yǐng*
fire	火	*huǒ*
fire exit	防火门	*fáng huǒ mén*
first aid	急救	*jí jiù*
fitting room	试衣间	*shì yī jiān*
flight	航班	*háng bān*
flu	流感	*liú gǎn*
food poisoning	食物中毒	*shí wù zhōng dú*
football	足球	*zú qiú*
for	为	*wéi*
form (document)	表格	*biǎo gé*
free	无人	*wú rén*
free (money)	免费	*miǎn fèi*
friend	朋友	*péng yǒu*
from	从	*cóng*

G

gallery	画廊	huà láng
garage	车库	chē kù
gas	汽油	qì yóu
gents (toilets)	男士	nán shì
girl	女孩	nǚ hái
glasses	眼镜	yǎn jìng
golf	高尔夫球	gāo ěr fū qiú
golf course	高尔夫球场	gāo ěr fū qiú chǎng

good/nice/ok/well 好 hǎo
hǎo (好), is a versatile word. Apart from "good", it can also mean "okay", as in "I've understood".

Great Wall	长城	cháng chéng
group	小组	xiǎo zǔ
guarantee	保证	bǎo zhèng
guide (person)	导游	dǎo yóu

H

hair	头发	tóu fa
hairdresser's	发廊	fà láng
half	半	bàn
heat	暖气	nuán qì
help!	救命！	jiù mìng!
here	这里	zhè lǐ
high	高	gāo
holiday (work-free day)	假日	jià rì
holidays	度假	dù jià
homosexual	同性恋	tóng xìng liàn
hospital	医院	yī yuàn
hot	热 (weather); 辣 (spicy)	rè (weather); là (spicy)
hotel	旅馆	lǚ guǎn
how?	怎么?	zěn me?
how big?	多大?	duō dà?
how far?	多远?	duō yuǎn?
how long?	多久?	duō jiǔ?
how much?	多少?	duō shǎo?
hurry up!	快走吧！	kuài zǒu ba!
husband	丈夫	zhàng fu

I

identity card	证件卡	zhèng jiàn kǎ
ill	病	bìng
immediately	立即	lì jí
important	重要	zhòng yào
in	在	zài

information	信息	xìn xí
inside	里面	lǐ miàn
insurance	保险	bǎo xiǎn

interesting 有趣 *yǒu qù*
This word can also go beyond "interesting". If you say *tā zhè ge rén hěn yǒu qù* (他这个人很有趣, he's an interesting person), you could imply that there's something intriguing about him.

international	国际	guó jì
internet	互联网	hù lián wǎng
Ireland	爱尔兰	ài ěr lán
Irish	爱尔兰人	ài ěr lán rén
island	海岛	hǎi dǎo
itinerary	日程	rì chéng

J

January	一月	yī yuè
jet ski	喷气式滑水板	pēn qì shì huá shuǐ bǎn
journey	旅途	lǚ tú
July	七月	qī yuè
junction	连接点	lián jiē diǎn
June	六月	liù yuè
just (only)	只	zhǐ

K

key	钥匙	yào shi
key ring	钥匙圈	yào shi quān
keyboard	键盘	jiàn pán
kid	儿童	ér tóng
kind (person)	亲切	qīn qiè
kind (sort)	种	zhǒng
kiosk	站	zhàn
kiss	亲吻	qīn wěn

L

label	标签	biāo qiān
ladies (toilets)	女	nǚ
lady	女士	nǚ shì
lake	湖	hú
language	语	yǔ
last	最后	zuì hòu
late (delayed)	晚点	wǎn diǎn
late (time)	晚了	wǎn le
launderette	洗衣店	xǐ yī diàn
lawyer	律师	lǜ shī
less	较少	jiào shǎo

library	图书馆	*tú shū guǎn*
life jacket	救生衣	*jiù shēng yī*
lifeguard	救生员	*jiù shēng yuán*
lift	电梯	*diàn tī*
to like	喜欢	*xǐ huān*
little	少许	*shǎo xǔ*
local	当地	*dāng dì*
to lose	丢失	*diū shī*
lost property	失物招领处	*shī wù zhāo lǐng chù*
luggage	行李	*xíng li*

M

madam	女士	*nǚ shì*
mail	邮件	*yóu jiàn*
main	主要	*zhǔ yào*
man	男人	*nán rén*
manager	经理	*jīng lǐ*
many	许多	*xǔ duō*
map (city)	地图	*dì tú*
map (road)	地图	*dì tú*
March	三月	*sān yuè*
market	市场	*shì chǎng*
married	结婚	*jié hūn*
May	五月	*wǔ yuè*
maybe	可能	*kě néng*
mechanic	技工	*jì gōng*
meeting	会议	*huì yì*
message	信息	*xìn xī*
midday	午间	*wǔ jiān*
midnight	午夜	*wǔ yè*
minimum	极小值	*jí xiǎo zhí*
minute	分钟	*fēn zhōng*
missing	不见	*bú jiàn*

---

mobile phone 手机 *shǒu jī*
China uses the same second-generation mobile
technology as the UK (GSM), so your phone should
work here if you've got roaming. Charges will be
exorbitant, though.

---

moment	分钟	*fēn zhōng*
money	钱	*qián*
more	更多	*gèng duō*
mosquito	蚊子	*wén zi*
most	最多	*zuì duō*
mother	母亲	*mǔ qīn*
much	多	*duō*
museum	博物馆	*bó wù guǎn*
musical	演奏	*yǎn zòu*

| must | 需要 | *xū yào* |
| my | 我的 | *wǒ de* |

N

name	名字	*míng zì*
nationality	国籍	*guó jí*
near	附近	*fù jìn*
necessary	必要	*bì yào*
never	从未	*cóng wèi*
new	新	*xīn*

| **news** | 新闻 | *xīn wén* |

International news channels, including CNN and BBC World, are available on cable or satellite. The most widely read English newspaper is the state-controlled China Daily.

newspaper	报纸	*bào zhǐ*
next	下一个	*xià yí gè*
next to	在旁边	*zài páng biān*
nice	好	*hǎo*
nice (people)	亲切	*qīn qiè*
night	夜里	*yè lǐ*
nightclub	夜总会	*yè zǒng huì*
north	北部	*běi bù*
note (money)	钞票	*chāo piào*
nothing	没什么	*méi shěn me*
November	十一月	*shí yī yuè*
now	现在	*xiàn zài*
nowhere	无处	*wú chù*
number	数字	*shù zì*

O

object	东西	*dōng xi*
October	十月	*shí yuè*
off (switched)	关	*guān*
office	办公室	*bàn gōng shī*
ok	好	*hǎo*
on	上	*shàng*
once	一次	*yí cì*
only	只	*zhǐ*
open	开着	*kāi zhe*
to open	打开	*dǎ kāi*
opera (Chinese)	戏曲	*xì qǔ*
opera (Western)	歌剧	*gē jù*
operator	接线员	*jiē xiàn yuán*
opposite (place)	相反	*xiāng fǎn*
optician's	验光店	*yàn guāng diàn*
or	或	*huò*

other	其他	*qí tā*
out of order	不可使用	*bù kě shǐ yòng*
outdoor	室外	*shì wài*
outside	外面	*wài miàn*
overnight	隔夜	*gé yè*
owner	所有者	*suǒ yǒu zhě*
oxygen	氧气	*yǎng qì*

P

painkiller	止痛药	*zhǐ tòng yào*
pair	双	*shuāng*
parents	父母	*fù mǔ*
park	公园	*gōng yuán*
parking	停车	*tíng chē*
party	聚会	*jù huì*
passport	护照	*hù zhào*
people	人们	*rén men*
perhaps	可能	*kě néng*
person	人	*rén*
petrol	汽油	*qì yóu*
photo	相片	*xiàng piàn*
phrase book	常用语手册	*cháng yòng yǔ shǒu cè*
place	地方	*dì fāng*
platform	站台	*zhàn tái*
police	警察	*jǐng chá*
port (sea)	口岸	*kǒu àn*
possible	可能	*kě néng*
post	邮件	*yóu jiàn*
post office	邮局	*yóu jú*

prescription 处方药 *chǔ fāng yào*
In Oriental medicine shops, just tell the herbalist what's ailing you and they'll recommend a cure. Note that dried and pounded animals, like seahorses, or animal parts may feature alongside the herbal content.

price	价格	*jià gé*
private	私有	*sī yǒu*
probably	大概	*dà gài*
problem	问题	*wèn tí*
pub	客栈	*kè zhàn*
public transport	公共交通工具	*gōng gòng jiāo tōng gōng jù*

Q

quality	质量	*zhì liàng*
quantity	数量	*shù liàng*
query	询问	*xún wèn*

question	问题	*wèn tí*
queue	队列	*duì liè*
quick	快	*kuài*
quickly	迅速	*xùn sù*
quiet	安静	*ān jìng*
quite	相当	*xiāng dāng*
quiz	测验	*cè yàn*

R

radio	收音机	*shōu yīn jī*
railway	铁路	*tiě lù*
rain	雨	*yǔ*
rape	强奸	*qiáng jiān*
ready	准备好	*zhǔn bèi hǎo*
real	真正	*zhēn zhèng*
receipt (shopping)	收据	*shōu jù*
reception	服务台	*fú wù tái*
receptionist	接待员	*jiē dài yuán*
reduction	减少	*jiǎn shǎo*
refund	退款	*tuì kuǎn*
to relax	放松	*fàng sōng*
rent	出租费	*chū zū fèi*
to rent	租	*zū*
reservation	预定	*yù dìng*

retired	退休	*tuì xiū*

You'll often see groups of senior citizens in parks doing tai chi, playing mah-jong, or just chatting over a cuppa. Dancing is increasingly popular, with little old couples practising their foxtrots in public.

rich	富有	*fù yǒu*
road	路	*lù*
room	房	*fáng*
route	路线	*lù xiàn*
rude	粗鲁	*cū lǔ*
ruins	废墟	*fèi xū*
to run	跑	*pǎo*

S

safe	保险柜 (box) 安全 (to be safe)	*bǎo xiǎn guì (box);* *ān quán (place)*
sauna	蒸气浴	*zhēng qì yù*
Scotland	苏格兰	*sū gé lán*
Scottish	苏格兰人	*sū gé lán rén*
sea	海	*hǎi*
seat	座位	*zuò wèi*
seat belt	安全带	*ān quán dài*
sedative	镇静剂	*zhèn jìng jì*

see you later!	再见！	*zài jiàn!*
self-service	自助	*zì zhù*
September	九月	*jiǔ yuè*
service	服务	*fú wù*
shop	商店	*shāng diàn*
shopping	购物	*gòu wù*
shopping centre	购物中心	*gòu wù zhōng xīn*
short	短小	*duǎn xiǎo*
to show	显示	*xiǎn shì*
shut	关闭	*guān bì*
sign	标志	*biāo zhì*
signature	署名	*shǔ míng*
since	从那以后	*cóng nà yǐ hòu*
sir	先生	*xiān shēng*
sister	姐妹	*jiě mèi*
ski	滑雪	*huá xuě*
sleeping pill	安眠药	*ān mián yào*
slow	慢	*màn*
small	小	*xiǎo*
soft	软	*ruǎn*
some	一些	*yì xiē*
something	某事	*mǒu shì*
son	儿子	*ér zi*
soon	很快	*hén kuài*
south	南部	*nán bù*
South Africa	南非	*nán fēi*
South African	南非人	*nán fēi rén*
speed	速度	*sù dù*
sport	体育	*tǐ yù*
stadium	体育场	*tǐ yù chǎng*
staff	职员	*zhí yuán*
stamp	邮票	*yóu piào*
station	站	*zhàn*
sterling pound	英镑	*yīng bàng*
straight	直	*zhí*
street	街道	*jiē dào*

stress	压力	*yā lì*

Acupuncture therapy is a traditional method of relieving stress and pain. It doesn't hurt and the general view is that when it's performed by a trained practitioner with sterile needles, it's perfectly safe.

suitcase	手提箱	*shǒu tí xiāng*
sun	太阳	*tài yáng*
sunblock	遮光剂	*zhē guāng jì*
sunglasses	太阳镜	*tài yáng jìng*
surname	姓氏	*xìng shì*
swimming pool	游泳池	*yóu yǒng chí*

| switched on | 接通 | *jiē tōng* |
| symptom | 症状 | *zhèng zhuàng* |

T

table	桌子	*zhuō zǐ*
to take	拿 (something); 吃药 (medicine)	*ná (something);* *chī yào (medicine)*
tampons	月经拴	*yuè jīng shuān*
tax	税	*shuì*
tax free	免税	*miǎn shuì*
taxi	出租车	*chū zū chē*
telephone	电话	*diàn huà*
telephone box	电话亭	*diàn huà tíng*
television	电视	*diàn shì*
temple	寺庙	*sì miào*
tennis	网球	*wǎng qiú*
tennis court	网球场	*wǎng qiú chǎng*
to text	发短信	*fā duǎn xìn*
that	那	*nà*
theft	偷窃	*tōu qiè*
then	然后	*rán hòu*
there	那里	*nà li*
thing	东西	*dōng xi*
to think	想	*xiǎng*
thirsty	渴	*kě*
this	这	*zhè*
through	通过	*tōng guò*
ticket (bus)	票	*piào*
ticket (cinema)	票	*piào*
ticket (parking)	违规停车罚单	*wéi guī tíng chē* *fá dān*
ticket office	售票处	*shòu piào chù*
time (clock)	时间	*shí jiān*
timetable	时间表	*shí jiān biǎo*
tip (money)	小费	*xiǎo fèi*
tired	累了	*lèi le*
to	到	*dào*
to (the left/right)	到（左/右边）	*dào (zuǒ/yòu biān)*
today	今天	*jīn tiān*
toilet	洗手间	*xǐ shǒu jiān*
toiletries	化妆品	*huà zhuāng pǐn*
toll	通行费	*tōng xíng fèi*
tomorrow	明天	*míng tiān*
tonight	今晚	*jīn wǎn*
too	太	*tài*
tourist office	旅游信息办公室	*lǚ yóu xìn xī bàn* *gōng shì*
town	镇	*zhèn*
train	火车	*huǒ chē*

tram	电车	*diàn chē*
to translate	翻译	*fān yì*
to travel	旅行	*lǚ xíng*
travel agency	旅行社	*lǚ xíng shè*
true (right)	对	*duì*
typical	典型	*diǎn xíng*

U

ulcer	溃疡	*kuì yáng*
umbrella	伞	*sǎn*
uncomfortable	难受	*nán shòu*
unconcious	没有知觉	*méi yǒu zhī jué*
under	下面	*xià miàn*
underground (tube)	地铁	*dì tiě*
to understand	理解	*lǐ jiě*
underwear	内裤	*nèi kù*
unemployed	失业者	*shī yè zhě*

unpleasant 令人不快 *lìng rén bú kuài*
Amongst the unpleasant foods that you might encounter, one that evokes much controversy is shark's fin (鱼翅, *yú chì*). You'll see this on just about every upmarket restaurant's menu, usually in the form of soup.

up	上	*shàng*
upstairs	在楼上	*zài lóu shàng*
urgent	迫切	*pò qiè*
to use	使用	*shǐ yòng*
useful	有用	*yǒu yòng*
usually	通常	*tōng cháng*

V

vacant	空房	*kōng fáng*
vacation	休假	*xiū jià*
vaccination	接种	*jiē zhòng*
valid	合法	*hé fǎ*
valuables	贵重物品	*guì zhòng wù pǐn*
value	价值	*jià zhí*
VAT	商品增值税	*shāng pǐn zēng zhí shuì*
vegetarian	素食者	*sù shí zhě*
vehicle	车辆	*chē liàng*
very	很	*hěn*
visa	签证	*qiān zhèng*
visit	参观	*cān guān*
to visit	参观	*cān guān*
vitamin	维生素	*wéi shēng sù*
to vomit	呕吐	*ǒu tù*

waiter/waitress	服务员/女服务员	*fú wù yuán/ nǔ fú wù yuán*
waiting room	候诊室	*hòu zhěn shì*
Wales	威尔士	*wēi ěr shì*
to walk	走	*zǒu*
wallet	钱包	*qián bāo*
to want	要	*yào*
to wash	洗	*xǐ*
watch	手表	*shǒu biǎo*
water	水	*shuǐ*
water sports	水上运动	*shuǐ shàng yùn dòng*
way (manner)	方式	*fāng shì*
way (route)	路线	*lù xiàn*
way in	入口	*rù kǒu*
way out	出口	*chū kǒu*
weather	天气	*tiān qì*
web	互联网	*hù lián wǎng*
website	网站	*wǎng zhàn*
week	星期	*xīng qī*
weekday	周日	*zhōu rì*
weekend	周末	*zhōu mò*
welcome	欢迎	*huān yíng*
well	好	*hǎo*
Welsh	威尔士人	*wēi ěr shì rén*
west	西部	*xī bù*
what?	什么?	*shén me?*
wheelchair	轮椅	*lún yǐ*
when?	什么时候?	*shén me shí hòu?*
where?	哪里?	*nǎ li?*
which?	哪些?	*nǎ xiē?*
while	当时	*dāng shí*
who?	谁?	*shuí?*
why?	为什么?	*wèi shén me?*
wife	妻子	*qī zi*

wine	酒	*jiǔ*

The Xinjiang region in northwestern China has ideal conditions for wine-growing, and there are some decent varieties, both red and white, being produced here.

with	跟	*gēn*
without	没有	*méi yǒu*
woman	妇女	*fù nǔ*
wonderful	美妙	*měi miào*
word	词	*cí*
work	工作	*gōng zuò*
to work (machine)	操作	*cāo zuò*

to work (person)	工作	*gōng zuò*
world	世界	*shì jiè*
worried	担心	*dān xīn*
to write	写	*xiě*
wrong (mistaken)	错误	*cuò wù*

X

| x-ray | X-射线 | *X-shè xiàn* |
| to x-ray | X-射线 | *X-shè xiàn* |

Y

yacht	游艇	*yóu tǐng*
year	年	*nián*
yearly	每年	*měi nián*
yellow pages	黄页	*huáng yè*
yes	是	*shì*
yesterday	昨天	*zuó tiān*
yet	尚未	*shàng wèi*

you (formal) 您 *nín*
Unlike some European languages, the formal "you"
is only brought out sparingly in Mandarin. You'll
encounter it in über-formal occasions, and it can
also be used as a term of respect towards the elderly.

you (informal)	你	*nǐ*
young	年轻	*nián qīng*
your (formal)	您的	*nín de*
your (informal)	你的	*nǐ de*
youth hostel	青年旅社	*qīng nián lǚ shè*

Z

zero	零	*líng*
zone	区域	*qū yù*
zoo	动物园	*dòng wù yuán*

Mandarin-English dictionary

A

ā sī pī lín	阿司匹林	aspirin
ài ěr lán	爱尔兰	Ireland
ài ěr lán rén	爱尔兰人	Irish
ài zī bìng	艾滋病	AIDS
ān quán	安全	safe (place)
ān jìng	安静	quiet
ān mián yào	安眠药	sleeping pill
ān pái	安排	to arrange
ān quán dài	安全带	seat belt
āng zāng	肮脏	dirty
ào zhōu	澳洲	Australia
ào zhōu rén	澳洲人	Australian

B

bā yuè	八月	**August**

Buddhist and Taoist traditions hold that the seventh month of the lunar calendar, which usually falls in August, is when the gates of the underworld open and the deceased visit the living.

bàn	半	half
bàn gōng shì	办公室	office
bàn lǐ dēng jī shǒu xù	办理登记手续	to check in (airport)
bàn rù zhù	办入住	to check in (hotel)
bǎo xiǎn	保险	insurance
bǎo xiǎn guì	保险柜	safe box
bào yuàn	抱怨	to complain
bǎo zhèng	保证	guarantee
bào zhǐ	报纸	newspaper
bèi bù	背部	back (body)
běi bù	北部	north
bì yào	必要	necessary
biǎo gé	表格	form (document)
biāo qiān	标签	label
biāo zhì	标志	sign
bié de	别的	another
bìng	病	ill
bó wù guǎn	博物馆	museum
bù hǎo	不好	bad
bù jiàn	不见	missing
bù kě shǐ yòng	不可使用	out of order

C

cān guān	参观	visit/to visit
cán jí	残疾	disabled
cāo zuò	操作	to work (machine)
cè yàn	测验	quiz
chā cuò	差错	error
cháng chéng	长城	Great Wall
cháng yòng yǔ shǒu cè	常用语手册	phrase book
chāo piào	钞票	note (money)
chē	车	car
chē kù	车库	garage
chē liàng	车辆	vehicle
chén liè	陈列	exhibition
chéng shì	城市	city
chī yào	吃药	to take medicine
chǔ fāng yào	处方药	prescription
chū kǒu	出口	exit
chū zū chē	出租车	taxi
chū zū fèi	出租费	rent
chuán rǎn	传染	contagious
cí	词	word
cóng	从	from
cóng nà yǐ hòu	从那以后	since
cóng wèi	从未	never
cū lǔ	粗鲁	rude
cuò wù	错误	wrong (mistaken)

D

dá	达	by (air, car, etc)
dà	大	big
dǎ diàn huà	打电话	to call/dial
dà gài	大概	probably

dà jiào táng	大教堂	**cathedral**

While temples might be a more common sight, there are also many churches and cathedrals catering to China's increasing Christian population.

dǎ kāi	打开	to open
dān xīn	担心	worried
dāng dì	当地	local
dāng shí	当时	while
dào	到	to
dào (zuǒ/yòu biān)	到（左/右边）	to (the left/right)
dǎo yóu	导游	guide (person)
dēng jī pái	登机牌	boarding card
dǐ dá	抵达	arrival

dì fāng	地方	place
dì tiě	地铁	metro (underground)
dì tú	地图	map
diàn chē	电车	tram
diàn huà	电话	telephone
diàn huà tíng	电话亭	telephone box
diàn nǎo	电脑	computer
diàn shì	电视	television
diàn tī	电梯	lift
diǎn xíng	典型	typical
diàn yǐng	电影	film (cinema)
diàn yǐng yuàn	电影院	cinema
diàn zǐ yǒu jiàn	电子邮件	e-mail
diū shī	丢失	to lose
dòng wù yuán	动物园	zoo
dōng xi	东西	object/thing
dú	毒	drug
dǔ bó yú lè chǎng	赌博娱乐场	casino
dù jià	度假	holidays
duǎn xiǎo	短小	short
duì	对	true (right)
duì huàn lǜ	兑换率	exchange rate

duì liè	队列	**queue**

Orderly queueing is not in the Chinese psyche, so be prepared to shove and be shoved. If you're too polite, you run the risk of not getting anything done.

duō	多	much
duō dà?	多大?	how big?
duō jiǔ?	多久?	how long?
duō shǎo?	多少?	how much?
duō yuǎn?	多远?	how far?

E

ér tóng	儿童	kid
èr yuè	二月	February
ér zi	儿子	son

F

fā duǎn xìn	发短信	to text
fà láng	发廊	hairdresser's
fān yì	翻译	to translate
fáng	房	room
fáng huǒ mén	防火门	fire exit
fāng shì	方式	way (manner)
fàng sōng	放松	to relax
fāng xiàng	方向	directions

fēi jī	飞机	aeroplane
fēi jī chǎng	飞机场	airport
fèi xū	废墟	ruins
fēn zhōng	分钟	minute/moment
fù jìn	附近	near
fù mǔ	父母	parents
fù nǚ	妇女	woman
fù qīn	父亲	father
fú wù	服务	service
fú wù tái	服务台	reception
fú wù yuán/	服务员/女服务员	waiter/waitress
nǚ fú wù yuán		
fù yǒu	富有	rich

G

gǎn mào	感冒	cold (illness)
gān rǎo	干扰	to disturb
gān xǐ	干洗	to dry clean
gān xǐ diàn	干洗店	dry cleaner's
gāo	高	high
gāo ěr fū qiú	高尔夫球	golf
gāo ěr fū qiú chǎng	高尔夫球场	golf course
gé yè	隔夜	overnight
gē jù	歌剧	opera (Western)
gēn	跟	with
gèng duō	更多	more
gèng hǎo	更好	better
gōng gòng jiāo tōng gōng jù	公共交通工具	public transport
gōng gòng qì chē	公共汽车	bus
gōng yù	公寓	apartment
gōng yuán	公园	park
gōng zuò	工作	work/to work (person)
gòu wù	购物	shopping
gòu wù zhōng xīn	购物中心	shopping centre
gù kè	顾客	customer
guān	关	off (switched)

guān bì	**关闭**	**closed/shut**

Most shops and department stores tend to close later than in Europe. Normal operating hours, especially for larger stores and boutiques, are approximately 9.30am to 9.30pm.

guān mén	关门	to close
guān shuì	关税	duty (tax)
guān yú	关于	about (concerning)

guāng pán/CD	光盘/CD	CD
guì zhòng wù pǐn	贵重物品	valuables
guó jí	国籍	nationality
guó jì	国际	international
guó jiā	国家	country
guò mǐn	过敏	allergy

H

hǎi	海	sea
hǎi àn	海岸	coast
hǎi dǎo	海岛	island
hǎi guān	海关	customs
hǎi tān	海滩	beach
hái zi	孩子	child
háng bān	航班	flight
háng kōng xìn	航空信	airmail
hǎo	好	good/nice/ok/well
hé	和	and
hé fǎ	合法	valid
hěn	很	very
hén kuài	很快	soon
hòu miàn	后面	back (place)
hòu zhěn shì	候诊室	waiting room
hú	湖	lake
hù lián wǎng	互联网	internet
hù zhào	护照	passport
huā fèi	花费	to cost
huà láng	画廊	gallery
huá xuě	滑雪	ski
huà zhuāng pǐn	化妆品	toiletries
huàn	换	to change
huān yíng	欢迎	welcome
huáng yè	黄页	yellow pages
huí dá	回答	to answer
huì yì	会议	meeting
huò	或	or
huǒ	火	fire

huò bì	货币	**currency**

The local currency is the *renminbi*, which literally means "people's currency". In everyday usage, it's known as the *yuan* (元).

huò bì duì huàn chù	货币兑换处	bureau de change
huǒ chē	火车	train

J

jì gōng	技工	mechanic

jí jiù	急救	first aid
jí xiǎo zhí	极小值	minimum
jí zhèng shì	急症室	A&E
jià gé	价格	price
jià rì	假日	holiday (work-free day)
jiā yóu zhàn	加油站	petrol station
jià zhí	价值	value
jiǎn	剪	to cut
jiàn pán	键盘	keyboard
jiǎn shǎo	减少	reduction
jiāo juǎn	胶卷	film (camera)
jiào shǎo	较少	less
jiē dài yuán	接待员	receptionist
jiē dào	街道	street
jié hūn	结婚	married
jiě mèi	姐妹	sister
jié rì	节日	festivals
jiē tōng	接通	switched on
jiē xiàn yuán	接线员	operator
jiē zhòng	接种	vaccination
jǐn jí zhuàng tài	紧急状态	emergency
jīn tiān	今天	today
jīn wǎn	今晚	tonight
jǐng chá	警察	police
jīng lǐ	经理	manager
jǐng zhōng	警钟	alarm
jiǔ	酒	wine
jiǔ bā	酒吧	bar (pub)
jiù hù chē	救护车	ambulance
jiù mìng!	救命！	help!
jiù shēng yī	救生衣	life jacket
jiù shēng yuán	救生员	lifeguard

jiǔ yuè	九月	**September**

The mid-autumn festival usually falls some time in September. Also known as the harvest festival, this is a time for families to honour the moon and eat mooncakes (*yuè bǐng*, 月饼), bean-filled sweet pastries.

jù huì	聚会	party
jù lè bù	俱乐部	club

K

kā fēi diàn	咖啡店	coffee house
kāi chē	开车	to drive
kāi zhe	开着	open
kào jìn	靠近	close by

kě	渴	thirsty
kě lì yòng	可利用	available
kě néng	可能	maybe
kě shì	可是	perhaps/possible/but

kě yǐ   可以   **can (to be able)**
The Chinese prefer not to decline a request directly.
You'll often hear *míng tiān ba* (明天吧, let's try tomorrow),
kǎo lù (考虑, I'll think about it), or *bù fāng biàn* (不方便,
that's not convenient).

kè zhàn	客栈	pub
kōng fáng	空房	vacant
kǒu àn	口岸	port (sea)
kuài	快	quick
kuài chē	快车	express (train)
kuài dì	快递	express (delivery)
kuài zi	筷子	chopsticks
kuài zǒu ba!	快走吧！	hurry up!
kuáng huān jié	狂欢节	carnival
kuì yáng	溃扬	ulcer
kùn nan	困难	difficult

L

là	辣	hot (spicy)
lèi le	累了	tired
lěng	冷	cold (temperature)
lì jí	立即	immediately
lǐ jiě	理解	to understand
lǐ miàn	里面	inside
lián jiē diǎn	连接点	junction
lián xì	联系	to contact
liáng	凉	cool
líng	零	zero
lìng rén bú kuài	令人不快	unpleasant
lǐng shì guǎn	领事馆	consulate
liú gǎn	流感	flu
liù yuè	六月	June
lù	路	road
lǚ guǎn	旅馆	hotel
lǜ shī	律师	lawyer
lǚ tú	旅途	journey
lù xiàn	路线	route
lǚ xíng	旅行	way (route)/to travel
lǚ xíng shè	旅行社	travel agency
lǚ yóu xìn xī bàn gōng shì	旅游信息办公室	tourist office
lún yǐ	轮椅	wheelchair

M

mǎi	买	to buy
màn	慢	slow
měi guó	美国	America
měi guó rén	美国人	American
měi miào	美妙	wonderful
měi nián	每年	yearly
méi shěn me	没什么	nothing
méi yǒu	没有	without
méi yǒu zhī jué	没有知觉	unconcious
miǎn fèi	免费	free (money)
miǎn shuì	免税	tax free
míng tiān	明天	tomorrow
míng zì	名字	name
mǒu shì	某事	something
mǔ qīn	母亲	mother

N

nà	那	that
ná	拿	to take (something)
nà li	那里	there
nǎ li?	哪里?	where?
nǎ xiē?	哪些?	which?
nǎi yóu	奶油	cream
nán bù	南部	south
nán fēi	南非	South Africa
nán fēi rén	南非人	South African
nán hái	男孩	boy
nán rén	男人	man
nán shì	男士	gents (toilets)
nán shòu	难受	uncomfortable
nèi kù	内裤	underwear
nǐ	你	you (informal)
nǐ de	你的	your (informal)
nián	年	year
nián qīng	年轻	young
nín	您	you (formal)
nín de	您的	your (formal)
nǚ ér	女儿	daughter
nǚ hái	女孩	girl
nǚ	女	ladies (toilets)
nǚ shì	女士	lady/madam
nuǎn qì	暖气	heat

O

ǒu tù	呕吐	to vomit

P

pǎo	跑	to run
pēn qì shì huá shuǐ bǎn	喷气式滑水板	jet ski

péng yǒu	**朋友**	**friend**

It's quite common to see two teenage girls holding hands. This is usually an expression of friendship; kissing in public is still taboo, though.

pián yí	便宜	cheap
piào	票	ticket
piào fáng	票房	box office
pò qiè	迫切	urgent

Q

qī jiān	期间	during
qí tā	其他	other
qì yóu	汽油	petrol
qī yuè	七月	July
qī zi	妻子	wife
qí zì xíng chē	骑自行车	cycling
qián	钱	money
qián bāo	钱包	wallet
qiān zhèng	签证	visa
qiáng jiān	强奸	rape
qīn qiè	亲切	kind (person)
qīn wěn	亲吻	kiss
qīng biàn xiǎo chuáng	轻便小床	cot
qīng nián lǚ shè	青年旅社	youth hostel
qū	区	area
qū hào	区号	area code
qǔ xiāo	取消	to cancel
qū yù	区域	zone
quán bù	全部	all
què rèn	确认	confirmation

R

rán hòu	然后	then
rè	热	hot (weather)
rén	人	person
rèn hé	任何	any
rén men	人们	people
rì chéng	日程	itinerary
rù kǒu	入口	entrance/way in
ruǎn	软	soft

S

săn	伞	umbrella
sān yuè	三月	March

> ### *shàng* 上 **on/up**
> To indicate location, you follow the noun with a location preposition. To say something is on a table, it's *zài zhuō zi shàng* (在桌子上), where *shàng* (上, on) comes after *zhuō zi* (桌子, table).

shāng diàn	商店	shop
shāng kŏu	伤口	cut
shāng pĭn zēng zhí shuì	商品增值税	VAT
shāng wù	商务	business
shāo	烧	to burn
shăo xŭ	少许	little
shè shī	设施	facilities
shén me shí hòu?	什么时候?	when?
shén me?	什么?	what?
shì	是	to be/yes
shì chăng	市场	market
shí èr yuè	十二月	December
shì gù	事故	accident
shĭ guăn	使馆	embassy
shí jiān	时间	time (clock)
shí jiān biăo	时间表	timetable
shì jiè	世界	world
shì wài	室外	outdoor
shī wù zhāo lĭng chù	失物招领处	lost property
shí wù zhōng dú	食物中毒	food poisoning
shī yè zhě	失业者	unemployed
shì yī jiān	试衣间	fitting room
shí yī yuè	十一月	November
shĭ yòng	使用	to use
shí yuè	十月	October
shŏu biăo	手表	watch
shōu fèi	收费	charge/to charge/cost
shŏu jī	手机	mobile phone
shōu jù	收据	receipt
shòu piào chù	售票处	ticket office
shŏu tí xiāng	手提箱	suitcase
shōu yīn jī	收音机	radio
shū	书	book
shù liàng	数量	quantity
shŭ míng	署名	signature
shù zì	数字	number (figure)

shuāng	双	double/pair
shuì	税	tax
shuǐ	水	water
shuǐ shàng yùn dòng	水上运动	water sports
shuí?	谁?	who?
sī jī	司机	driver
sī jī jià zhào	司机驾照	driving licence
sī yǒu	私有	private
sì miào	寺庙	temple
sì yuè	四月	April
sù dù	速度	speed
sū gé lán	苏格兰	Scotland
sū gé lán rén	苏格兰人	Scottish
sù shí zhě	素食者	vegetarian
sǔn shāng	损伤	damage
suǒ yǒu zhě	所有者	owner

T

tài	太	too
tài yáng	太阳	sun
tài yáng jìng	太阳镜	sunglasses
tǐ yù	体育	sport
tǐ yù chǎng	体育场	stadium
tiān	天	day
tiān qì	天气	weather
tiě lù	铁路	railway
tíng chē	停车	parking
tōng cháng	通常	usually
tōng guò	通过	by (via)/through
tōng xíng fèi	通行费	toll

tóng xìng liàn	同性恋	**homosexual**

The Chinese are tolerant of homosexuality, and there is no explicit law against it. In the larger cities, the gay scene – bars, clubs, teahouses, saunas – is fairly open.

tóu fa	头发	hair
tōu qiè	偷窃	theft
tú shū guǎn	图书馆	library
tuì kuǎn	退款	refund
tuì xiū	退休	retired
tuō shuǐ	脱水	to dehydrate

W

wài miàn	外面	outside
wǎn diǎn	晚点	delay/late
wǎng qiú	网球	tennis
wǎng qiú chǎng	网球场	tennis court

wǎng zhàn	网站	website
wéi	为	for
wēi ěr shì	威尔士	Wales
wēi ěr shì rén	威尔士人	Welsh
wéi guī tíng chē fá dān	违规停车罚单	ticket (parking)
wèi shén me?	为什么?	why?
wéi shēng sù	维生素	vitamin
wēi xiǎn	危险	danger
wèn	问	to ask
wèn tí	问题	problem/question
wén zi	蚊子	mosquito
wǒ de	我的	my
wú chù	无处	nowhere
wǔ jiān	午间	midday
wú rén	无人	free
wǔ yè	午夜	midnight
wǔ yuè	五月	May

X

xǐ	洗	to wash
xī bù	西部	west
xì qǔ	戏曲	opera (Chinese)
xǐ huān	喜欢	to like
xǐ shǒu jiān	洗手间	toilet
xǐ yī diàn	洗衣店	launderette
xià	下	down
xià miàn	下面	under
xià yí gè	下一个	next
xiàn jīn	现金	cash
xiān shēng	先生	sir
xiǎn shì	显示	to show
xiàn zài	现在	now
xiǎng	想	to think
xiāng dāng	相当	quite
xiāng fǎn	相反	opposite (place)
xiàng piàn	相片	photo
xiāng xià	乡下	countryside
xiāng yān	香烟	cigarette
xiǎo	小	small
xiǎo cān guǎn	小餐馆	café
xiǎo fèi	小费	tip (money)

xiǎo zǔ	小组	group
xiě	写	to write
xīn	新	new
xīn wén	新闻	news
xìn xī	信息	information/message
xìn yòng kǎ	信用卡	credit card
xíng / hǎo le	行/ 好了	all right
xíng li	行李	baggage/luggage
xīng qī	星期	week
xìng shì	姓氏	surname
xiōng dì	兄弟	brother
xiū jià	休假	vacation
X-shè xiàn	X-射线	x-ray/to x-ray
xǔ duō	许多	many
xū yào	需要	must
xuǎn zé	选择	to choose
xuě jiā	雪茄	cigar
xùn sù	迅速	quickly
xún wèn	询问	query

Y

yā lì	压力	stress
yàn guāng diàn	验光店	optician's
yǎn jìng	眼镜	glasses
yán sè	颜色	colour
yǎn zòu	演奏	musical
yǎng qì	氧气	oxygen
yào	要	to want
yào shi	钥匙	key
yào shi quān	钥匙圈	key ring
yè	夜	night
yè zǒng huì	夜总会	nightclub
yí cì	一次	once
yì diǎn	一点	bit (a)

yí gè	一个	**a(n)**

A more accurate translation of *yí gè* (一个) is "one", as Mandarin doesn't use articles. But there are measure words, which are similar to collective nouns in English.

yǐ qián	以前	ago
yī shēng	医生	doctor
yì shù	艺术	art
yī wù	衣物	clothes
yì xiē	一些	some
yī yuàn	医院	hospital
yī yuè	一月	January
yīn wèi	因为	because

yīng bàng	英镑	sterling pound

yīng guó	英国	England
yīng guó rén	英国人	English (person)
yīng yǔ	英语	English (language)
yóu jiàn	邮件	mail/post
yóu jú	邮局	post office
yóu piào	邮票	stamp
yǒu qù	有趣	interesting
yóu tǐng	游艇	yacht
yǒu yòng	有用	useful
yóu yǒng chí	游泳池	swimming pool
yóu yú	由于	because of
yǔ	语	language
yǔ	雨	rain
yù dìng	预定	to book/booking/ reservation
yù gāng	浴缸	bath
yuǎn	远	far
yuàn yán	怨言	complaint
yuē huì	约会	appointment
yuè jīng shuān	月经拴	tampons

Z

zài	再	again
zài	在	at (time)/in
zài fù jìn	在附近	around
zài jiàn!	再见！	see you later!
zài lóu shàng	在楼上	upstairs
zài páng biān	在旁边	by (beside)/next to
zài zhī jiān	在之间	between
zǎo	早	early
zěn me?	怎么?	how?
zhàn	站	kiosk/station
zhàn tái	站台	platform
zhàng dān	账单	bill
zhàng fu	丈夫	husband
zhào xiàng jī	照相机	camera
zhè	这	this
zhē guāng jì	遮光剂	sunblock
zhé kòu	折扣	discount
zhè lǐ	这里	here

zhèn	镇	town
zhèn jìng jì	镇静剂	sedative
zhēn zhèng	真正	real
zhèng jiàn kǎ	证件卡	identity card
zhēng qì yù	蒸气浴	sauna
zhèng què	正确	exactly
zhèng shí	证实	to confirm
zhèng zhuàng	症状	symptom
zhí	直	straight
zhǐ	只	just/only
zhì liàng	质量	quality
zhī piào	支票	cheque
zhǐ tòng yào	止痛药	painkiller
zhí yuán	职员	staff
zhǒng	种	kind (sort)
zhōng xīn	中心	centre
zhòng yào	重要	important
zhōu mò	周末	weekend
zhōu nián jì niàn	周年纪念	anniversary
zhōu rì	周日	weekday
zhù sù	住宿	accommodation
zhǔ yào	主要	main
zhǔn bèi hǎo	准备好	ready
zhuō zǐ	桌子	table
zì dòng qǔ kuǎn jī	自动取款机	cash point
zì xíng chē	自行车	bicycle
zì zhù	自助	self-service
zǒu	走	to walk
zū	租	to rent
zú gòu	足够	enough
zú qiú	足球	football
zuì ài	最爱	favourite
zuì duō	最多	most
zuì hǎo	最好	best
zuì hòu	最后	last

zuì xíng	罪行	**crime**

The crime rate is comparatively low, but tourists should still watch out for pickpockets, who sometimes work in stores in complicity with security guards.

zuó tiān	昨天	yesterday
zuò wèi	座位	seat

Quick reference

Numbers

0	零	*líng*
1	一	*yī*
2	二	*èr*
3	三	*sān*
4	四	*sì*
5	五	*wǔ*
6	六	*liù*
7	七	*qī*
8	八	*bā*
9	九	*jiǔ*
10	十	*shí*
11	十一	*shí yī*
12	十二	*shí ér*
13	十三	*shí sān*
14	十四	*shí sì*
15	十五	*shí wǔ*
16	十六	*shí liù*
17	十七	*shí qī*
18	十八	*shí bā*
19	十九	*shí jiǔ*
20	二十	*èr shí*
21	二十一	*èr shí yī*
30	三十	*sān shí*
40	四十	*sì shí*
50	五十	*wǔ shí*
60	六十	*liù shí*
70	七十	*qī shí*
80	八十	*bā shí*
90	九十	*jiǔ shí*
100	一百	*yì bǎi*
1000	一千	*yì qiān*
1st	第一	*dì yī*
2nd	第二	*dì èr*
3rd	第三	*dì sān*
4th	第四	*dì sì*
5th	第五	*dì wǔ*

Weights & measures

gram (=0.03oz)	克	*kè*
kilogram (=2.2lb)	公斤	*gōng jīn*
pound (=0.45kg)	磅	*bàng*
centimetre (=0.4in)	厘米	*lí mǐ*
metre (=1.1yd)	米	*mǐ*
kilometre (=0.6m)	公里	*gōng lǐ*
litre (=2.1pt)	公升	*gōng shēng*

Days & time

Monday	星期一	*xīng qī yī*
Tuesday	星期二	*xīng qī èr*
Wednesday	星期三	*xīng qī sān*
Thursday	星期四	*xīng qī sì*
Friday	星期五	*xīng qī wǔ*
Saturday	星期六	*xīng qī liù*
Sunday	星期天	*xīng qī tiān*

What time is it?	几点了？	*jǐ diǎn le?*
(Four) o'clock	(四)点	*(sì) diǎn*
Quarter past (six)	(六点)一刻	*(liù diǎn) yí kè*
Half past (eight)	(八点)半	*(bā diǎn) bàn*
Quarter to (ten)	差一刻(到十点)	*chà yí kè (dào shí diǎn)*

morning	上午	*shàng wǔ*
afternoon	下午	*xià wǔ*
evening	晚上	*wǎn shàng*
night	夜里	*yè lǐ*

Clothes size conversions

Women's clothes	34	36	38	40	42	44	46	50
equiv. UK size	6	8	10	12	14	16	18	20

Men's jackets	44	46	48	50	52	54	56	58
equiv. UK size	34	36	38	40	42	44	46	48

Men's shirts	36	37	38	39	40	41	42	43
equiv. UK size	14	14.5	15	15.5	16	16.5	17	17.5

Shoes	36.5	37.5	39	40	41.5	42.5	44	45
equiv. UK size	4	5	6	7	8	9	10	11